Your grow-a-loaf guidebook

Chris Young and the Real Bread Campaign

Contents

Introduction — 4
What is Real Bread? — 7
About the Real Bread Campaign — 8

Grow — 11
Wheat — 11
Where to get wheat seeds — 15
Where to grow your wheat — 19
Sowing — 21
Caring for your crop — 25

Mill — 29
Harvesting — 29
Threshing — 32
Winnowing — 32
Milling — 33

Bake — 39
Ingredients — 39
Equipment — 42
Techniques — 46
Recipes — 51
Sourdough bread — 58
Storing bread — 64

Field notes — 67
Bakers' Bush — 67
Playing fields of wheat — 68
Seed to sandwich in Shaky Toon — 70
From seed to sourdough — 72

Contents

Lessons in Loaf   **75**
Indoor wheat growing   75
How does your garden grow?   77
Yeast balloons   78
Gluten washing   79
Farming methods   81
What is Real Bread?   83
How are different products made?   85
A slice of history   88
Healthy eating   89
Health and safety   92
The evolution of traditional milling   93
Modern milling   96
Comparing different milling methods   97
In praise of wholemeal   100
The language of loaf   101
An A to Z of Real Bread   104
Bread from around the world   108
Further notes for teachers   112
Example lesson plans   113
Who'll run your Real Breadmaking session?   116
UK bakery market   118
Historical authenticity   119
Chemical raising agents   120

Wheat diaries   **123**

Find out more   **139**

Roll of honour   **145**

Introduction

Mmm, Real Bread! How much time have you ever spent thinking about where it comes from? I don't just mean from a bakery but right back to the grain growing in a farmer's field. Lots of time? Some? None? Well, whatever, **Bake Your Lawn** is here to help you guide children in taking a handful of wheat and growing their own Real Bread.

A square metre of soil and barely a child's handful of wheat seeds should be space and grain enough to produce flour for a small loaf. If you have access to more space, go for it! If you have less space, you can at least grow some wheat in a flowerpot or planter to follow its life cycle.

This book builds on the Bake Your Lawn and Lessons in Loaf projects that we created and ran from 2010 to 2012. They helped thousands of school children not only to follow the journey from crop to crust but also discover the connections that bread has with almost every aspect of learning and life in general. Seeing photos of beaming children with Real Bread they'd grown is still a highlight of my decade and a half on the Campaign trail.

As a topic, Real Bread is an absolute gift to teachers. It can be used in pretty much every subject across the curriculum: ancient and modern foreign languages; art and design; citizenship; computing; design and technology; English; geography; health education; history; maths; music; personal, social and health education; religion; science subjects... Maybe not PE, unless you count all that digging, threshing and whatnot. On the music front, there are loads of songs to be sung about the whole process, from tilling to toast.

The level of detail in this book should be more than enough for children of all ages, abilities and levels of interest, allowing you to filter, select and present as appropriate to the young'uns in your charge. There's a chance you might even discover a thing or two yourself.

The book's title came from Real Bread Campaign co-founder Andrew Whitley, who really did bake his lawn. Sort of. Back in the 1970s, before anyone talked much about urban agriculture, Andrew turned his allotment in Stoke Newington's Clissold Park into a mini wheatfield, from which he produced his own Real Bread. Following the Village Bakery and Bread Matters years, Andrew has fully re-connected with the soil-to-slice ethos and is a figurehead in the UK's non-commodity grain revival through his Scotland the Bread work.

Intro

Bake Your Lawn is a companion to **Slow Dough: Real Bread**, in which you can find around 90 recipes; and **Knead to Know...more**, our handbook for setting up a microbakery.

Happy growing, milling, baking and eating,

Chris Young, Penge, February 2024

PS If it all goes thingies up at any point, please don't get too disheartened. You can grab a bag of grain or flour that someone else has produced and hop on the seed to sandwich journey from that point.

Disclaimer

Bake Your Lawn is intended as guidance only and is to be read in conjunction with your own independent research. Sustain cannot be held responsible for the results of following any suggestions it contains. We have made reasonable efforts to ensure accuracy of the information and whilst we apologise for any errors or omissions, cannot be held responsible for any consequences that might arise because of them.

Awareness of, and compliance with, legislation applicable in your part of the world is your responsibility and you should check with the relevant authorities to ensure that you fulfil these obligations. When organising and running any practical projects (planting, harvesting, oven building, baking, experimenting and serving up food to eat, for example) you should always ensure that you have taken adequate precautions to ensure the health and safety of everyone involved.

Inclusion in Bake Your Lawn of any organisation, individual, product or service is not necessarily an endorsement and does not imply one. Any view expressed in this publication is that of the person quoted and not necessarily that of the Real Bread Campaign or Sustain. Conversely, not everyone named in the book necessarily agrees with everything we have said in it.

If you have feedback that you feel would enhance any future editions of Bake Your Lawn, please email it to **realbread@sustainweb.org**

At a glance

The key stages we cover in this book are:

Grow

- Getting your hands on wheat seeds.
- Preparing a seed bed.
- Planting.
- Caring for your crop.

Mill

- Harvesting.
- Threshing to separate the grains from the stems.
- Winnowing grain to remove the chaff.
- Grinding grain.
- Sieving and maturing flour.

Bake

- More about flour and other ingredients.
- Equipment.
- Using your flour to make the tastiest Real Bread ever.

Field notes

- Stories from grow-a-loaf school projects.

Lessons in Loaf

- Some simple experiments to try at home or in school.
- Thinking about how bread fits into the school timetable and life in general.

Wheat diaries

- Further inspiration from folk who took part in the Real Bread Campaign's original Lessons in Loaf and Bake Your Lawn projects.

What is Real Bread?

As everyone has their own idea of what Real Bread is, here's our basic definition: Real Bread is made without chemical raising agents (such as baking powder), so-called processing aids or any other additives.*

Simple, eh? That's because it is! Sadly, perhaps around 95% or more of what is sold as 'bread' in the UK falls short of this very low bar – see page 118.

Everything, everyone, everywhere

Real Bread isn't a look, shape or style. Contrary to some people's understanding, Real Bread doesn't necessarily have to be made by the sourdough process or by artisan bakers, and it can be made using gluten-free flour.

Real Bread is made and enjoyed by people of every age, nationality, colour, sex, sexual orientation, gender identity, ethnic heritage, differing ability, neurological status, religion, economic background, who collectively speak all languages worldwide.

Our universally inclusive definition encompasses every type of additive-free bread made from every type of flour – whether baked, steamed, fried, roasted or griddled – by artisans and amateurs alike. From Agege, baguette, bao, bap, bara brith, bialy, challah, chapatti, ciabatta, injera, khobez, lavash, naan, paratha, pide, pitta, roti, ruisleipä, shokupan, Staffordshire oatcake, stottie, tortilla to zopf, the A to Z of what can be Real Bread** goes on around the globe.

*The only exceptions we make are for so-called 'fortificants' in places where their addition is mandatory: to most flour in the UK, for example – see page 99.

**Though, sadly, some manufacturers choose to use additives, putting their products outside our definition.

About the Real Bread Campaign

Since November 2009, the Real Bread Campaign has been finding and sharing ways of making bread better for us, better for our communities and better for the planet. We champion Real Bread and the people who make it, while challenging obstacles to their rise. The Campaign works towards a future in which everyone has the chance to choose Real Bread and can get it within walking or cycling distance. In some cases this will be as close as bread made (and even grown) at home.

The Campaign is run by the charity Sustain: the alliance for better food and farming. We created it with baker and activist Andrew Whitley, who is also the co-founder of Bread Matters and Scotland the Bread.

Share your photos

We'd love to see your photos of lawn bakers in action – growing, milling, baking and eating their own Real Bread.

#RealBread #RealBreadCampaign #BakeYourLawn

Instagram and Facebook: **@realbreadcampaign** Twitter: **@realbread**

You can also email your photos to us: **realbread@sustainweb.org**

Before sending your photos or posting them online, please check with the person/people in them (or their legal guardian, if they're under 18) that they give permission for their image to be published. We may use photos we receive to help publicise our charity's work. Please also let us know the name of the person or organisation to be credited for the photograph if we use it.

Grow

Real Bread can be made from all sorts of things (see page 87) but because most in the UK is made from wheat, that's what this book focuses on.

Please don't be daunted! As with the rest of the book, this section goes into far more detail than you'll probably need for a small-scale project. What it basically says is that all you need is to find a patch of soil, chuck a handful of wheat seeds at it, cover them and leave the plants to grow.

Wheat

Wheat is a type of grass. Though maize takes the global top crop spot based on weight produced, wheat fields cover more of the earth's surface than any other grain.

The scientific name for common (aka modern or bread) wheat, which is the stuff most often used to make bread (plus biscuits, cakes, pastry and whatnot) in the UK, is *Triticum aestivum*. There are umpteen cultivars, or varieties, of *T. aestivum*. Each differs in yield (how much grain the plant from each seed will produce), protein and vitamin content, cooking qualities (e.g. whether better for bread or cakes), flavour and so on.

Almost every wheat field you see is planted with a single variety. This will have been selected from a limited number that are widely available to farmers and usually from an even smaller list of varieties recommended each season by the UK farming industry's Agriculture and Horticulture Development Board.

The wheat plant

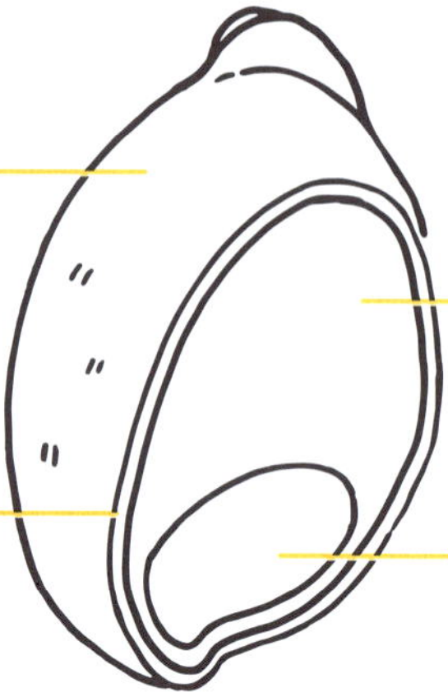

- Bran
- Endosperm
- Aleurone
- Germ

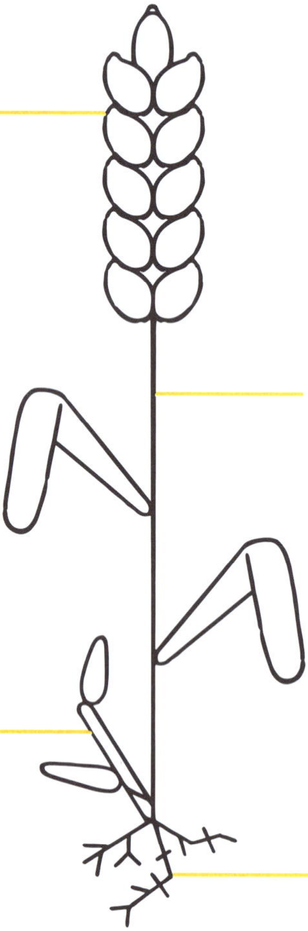

- Ear
- Stem
- Tiller
- Roots

Berry

The wheat berry, also known as the kernel, seed or grain, is the bit of most interest to the baker as this is where flour comes from. It consists of three main parts:

- Endosperm.
- Germ.
- Bran.

The endosperm takes its name from the ancient Greek for 'inside the seed'. It's the whitish part of the wheat berry, accounting for about 85% of its weight. It's mainly carbohydrate and protein, which provide a lot of what the wheat plant needs in the earliest stages of growth. In breadmaking, they're the key building blocks of dough.

The germ is the embryo from which a new wheat plant grows. Although small (only about 2% of the wheat berry by weight), this oily part of the grain is packed with vitamins (notably vitamin E), minerals and some protein.

The bran is the tough, multi-layered outer casing that protects the wheat berry. As well as being where most of the fibre in wheat is concentrated, it's also rich in minerals. Between the endosperm and bran is the aleurone layer, which contains high levels of vitamins, minerals (including phosphorus in the form of phytate), protein and oils.

Ear

The cluster of wheat berries at the top of the stem is known as the ear, head or spike. It contains between around 16 to 25 spikelets, each made up of two or three wheat berries.

Each berry is covered by a protective hull, also known as a glume. Some 'bearded' varieties of wheat have long barbed awns on the glumes, which they inherited from their wild ancestors. These provide some protection from bird attack and in hot climates can help to hold moisture around the berry and reduce the risk of it drying out. Most varieties grown in cooler places, like the UK, have been bred to have very short awns or none at all.

Stem

The stem is the main stalk of the wheat plant, which supports the ear and transports nutrients to the wheat berries After the wheat is harvested, the dried, golden-coloured stems are known as straw. Straw can be ploughed into the ground to return nutrients to the soil or be put to other uses, such as bedding for animals or insulation for buildings.

Tiller

In addition to the central stem, a wheat plant may have side stems called tillers, though not all will survive to produce seed heads. Some varieties produce more tillers than others, while winter sowing gives a plant more time to produce them.

Roots

The roots anchor the wheat plant in the ground and draw in water and nutrients to feed it. The wheat plant has two types of roots. The primary root system, called the seminal roots, grow from the seed and help to nourish the wheat seedling. The secondary, or nodal, roots grow later on and provide stability for the main stem and tillers.

How much wheat do you need?

Depending on your method of sowing (see pages 21 to 24), you will need no more than about 50g (and perhaps as little as 15g) of wheat seeds per square metre.

How big a lawn to bake bread for a year?

Back in 2008, the BBC News website asked Real Bread Campaign co-founder Andrew Whitley how much space someone would need to make enough Real Bread to supply a family of four for a year. Based on a statistic from earlier in the decade that people in the UK each ate an average of 720g of bread a week, Andrew estimated an area of about 297 square metres would grow enough wheat. That would produce about 90kg of wholemeal flour, which at 432g of flour per 720g loaf would make 208 loaves – one per person per week for 52 weeks. The article noted that the charity Garden Organic had said the average British lawn was only about 90 square metres.

A much smaller area than 297 square metres might be sufficient, though. Yields of wheat vary greatly, depending on many factors including the soil type and health, annual weather conditions, fertilisers used (or not), loss to pests, previous crops in the field and more. A square metre might produce as little as 100g or as much as 1,000g of wheat, though the average produced by organic farmers in the UK seems to be about four to five tonnes per hectare – 400-500g per square metre. Consumption of bread also varies between people – for example, children in that fictional family of four might eat far less than 720g of bread a week.

When to plant

In the UK, varieties are classed as either spring or winter wheat, depending on when they are best sown. When choosing seed, it's important to check you're getting a variety most suited for sowing at the time of year you plan to plant it.

Winter wheat should be sown early in the season, usually between October and the end of November. After an initial growth phase, it needs a period with fairly consistent temperatures between about 1°C and 7°C to trigger growth, a process known as vernalisation. Winter wheat has the advantage of getting a head start on weeds before a growth pause in mid-winter, ready for the main race when the longer, warmer days come along in spring.

Spring wheat should be sown once the soil is over about 8°C. Don't worry about getting your thermometer out – depending where you are in the UK and what the winter/spring is like, the window is usually from about February through to the end of March. Some varieties can be sown as late as April, while in some years and places (Scotland, for example), sowing might need to be held back until early May.

Whether you plant winter or spring wheat, if you are growing in the UK then your crop should be ready to harvest at the end of the summer or early autumn, usually during July or August. Harvest time might come later in colder years or cooler parts of the UK – spring varieties sown in Scotland are sometimes only ready in September. If you are growing elsewhere in the world, timings will be different.

Where to get wheat seeds

This can be tricky. Wheat isn't a plant you tend to find amongst the small packets of seeds sold to gardeners. Places from which you might be able to obtain wheat seeds include a:

- local cereal farm.
- working, traditional flour mill.
- Real Bread bakery with a small-scale mill.
- seed bank.
- local seed swap / exchange group.
- website. Search for 'bread wheat seeds' or 'milling wheat' as a lot of what we found is intended to be grown as wheat shoots/grass for juicing or for cats, and the sellers didn't know what varieties they were offering.

Some people behind the first three of these categories are involved in the UK's growing number of local/regional non-commodity grain networks. Though agricultural seed merchants are set up to deal in huge, farm-sized orders, you could try asking if one will let you buy a small amount of wheat.

Which wheat to choose

Like any living thing, there isn't just one type of wheat and not all types of wheat (or even varieties of *T. aestivum*) are ideal for breadmaking. Some are better for making cakes and biscuits and some are best suited as animal feed. To give you the best chance of success growing and making Real Bread from your wheat, check with your supplier:

- that the variety is suitable for breadmaking.
- the time of year it's supposed to be sown.
- it has been cleaned and stored properly.
- that it hasn't been treated with any chemicals.

Hard or soft, weak or strong?

In simple terms, hard wheat has a harder kernel and soft wheat has a softer one. Unless you're planning to become a miller or cereal farmer, it's not something you really need to think about.

What's more important to a baker is how 'strong' or 'weak' a batch of wheat (and flour milled from it) is. Strong wheat has a higher protein content, usually 11-13% or more. As well as the quantity of protein, its quality is important. Strong flours tend have more elastic proteins, which produce dough that springs back and is well suited to many types of bread.

The term weak is used for wheat (and flour) that has less protein, sometimes below 10%, that is more extensible: stretchy rather than springy. Weaker flours are better suited to making cakes, biscuits and pastry, or for thickening sauces. They are often sold as 'plain', 'cake', or 'all purpose' flours.

All that said, you can make bread with lower protein, 'weaker' flours. They are better-suited to flatbreads and other types that don't require a high rise - baguette, ciabatta, crumpets and focaccia, for example. Treated right (see stretch and fold notes on pages 46 and 47) they can also be used to make bigger loaves.

Organic wheat

The world's largest seed breeders are multinational chemical companies, so it's perhaps no surprise that many modern varieties of wheat are heavily reliant on artificial fertilisers, herbicides, insecticides and other agrochemical inputs to thrive. As you won't be using any of these, you might find that you get better results with varieties of wheat that have been bred specifically to grow in organic farming conditions. Older varieties, dating back to before the boom of agrochemicals in

the wake of the Second World War, were bred to be grown by 'organic' farming by default. Don't worry if all you can find is a modern variety, bred for 'conventional' farming, though!

Comparing older and newer wheats

Many pre-20th century (sometimes known as 'heritage' or 'heirloom') varieties of bread wheat have very long stems, some as tall as people. Historically, this long straw was valuable for several uses, including as thatching for roofs. Since the mid-20th century, most wheat varieties have been bred to have much shorter stems, partly so that when synthetic fertiliser is applied, they are less likely to fall over. This also allows the plant to concentrate more of its energy and nutrition on developing the berries to increase the yield – the volume of wheat harvested. One drawback is that shorter stems allow more light to reach the ground, which favours the growth of weeds. This is one of the reasons that cultivation of modern, dwarf varieties of wheat tend to be highly dependent on the use of chemical herbicides. Another unintended consequence of the drive for higher yields and protein content/quality has been a general reduction in micronutritional quality of wheat.

In the UK, there is no legal definition of heritage or heirloom and people don't all agree on when the cutoff date should be. Some include varieties bred up to the middle of the 20th century, for example.

Seed saving

In the UK and many other countries, each wheat (or any food crop) field you see is likely to be planted with seeds of a single variety, which were bought for sowing that year. This isn't the way things were always done. Farmers and other growers used to clean and save some seeds from one year's harvest to sow the following year, and perhaps pass or sell some on to other growers to help them out and maybe make a little bit of money.

Seed saving is still common in some parts of the world but current seed marketing regulations (see below) in many countries, including the UK, make the practice difficult. Another deterrent is that seed companies assert corporate intellectual property rights over varieties they develop, which can only be grown under licences that tend to prohibit seed saving. The companies can threaten (and some take) legal action against farmers growing trademarked grain varieties outside the licensing conditions. This helps to ensure regular income for the companies from farmers buying licensed seed each year.

Mixed populations and landraces

Crossbreeding a number of single varieties will produce what's known as population wheat. Farmers and seed breeders might choose to create a population by selecting parent varieties that have a range of desired qualities, such as resistance to drought, high yield or being good for breadmaking. Unlike most modern farm fields, the plants in a crop of population wheat are genetically diverse and might look quite different from each other.

When a plant variety or population is grown in the same area for generations, it might adapt to the local soil, climate and other growing conditions, becoming what is known as a landrace. Landraces tend to be fairly resilient, especially those that are genetically diverse populations. Different varieties in the crop will do well or struggle each year, depending on the weather, diseases and so on. The diversity helps reduces the risk of disease and pest epidemics, lessens the risk of total crop failure, and contributes to fairly consistent yields year-on-year.

Seed marketing regulations

The law by which seeds can be made available to farmers means that it can be hard to get hold of populations, landraces and older varieties for agricultural use. As long as your Bake Your Lawn project is non-commercial (meaning you won't be selling the wheat you grow) you might find it slightly easier to find small quantities of varieties that aren't on the Great Britain and Northern Ireland nationals lists of permitted varieties. This can also make the story behind your wheat (and the Real Bread it produces) all the more interesting.

Drawing the short straw

A drawback of short stems is that they allow more light to reach the ground, which favours the growth of weeds. The 'conventional' farming answer is to apply herbicides (chemical weedkillers) but the result is that the only plants left in the field are wheat, which isn't great for biodiversity. Modern wheat varieties are typically genetically homogeneous and only a handful of closely related varieties dominate what is sown across whole countries and continents. This creates a higher risk of epidemic-scale disease and pest problems. In modern industrial (sometimes known as 'conventional') farming, yet more agrochemicals (fungicides and pesticides) are thrown into the environment and food chain, often pre-emptively – before a problem arises.

Where to grow your wheat

Your sowing site can be at ground level or in a raised bed. Soil in a raised bed might have better drainage and warm up a little earlier than at ground level, which can be useful for spring sowing. Ideally, your plot should receive full sunlight and not be sheltered from rain, though some shelter from wind can be useful.

Try to select a plot with good quality, medium-heavy topsoil, which will help to reduce the risk of the wheat plants lodging (falling over – see page 26) compared to growing in very sandy soils. Although wheat can grow in quite shallow ground, its roots can grow to over 40cm long. To allow good anchoring and reduce the risk of drying out, it's best to ensure the soil is at least 25cm deep.

To reduce your workload, try to avoid sowing your wheat in a place that has a problem with 'difficult' weeds, which you'd need to dig out before sowing and again during the growing season. If you plan on running your project in consecutive years, see the crop rotation notes on page 81.

Planters

If you don't have access to a plot of land you can dig up, but still have some outdoor space, then you can grow wheat in a planter. This might involve building a small, raised bed, or buying / getting your hands on a large planter or something that can be used as one. We heard from one inner-city school who made theirs from a heavy-duty polythene drum, which they cut in half and set up in a corner of the playground.

Building a raised bed

If you have, or know someone with, bricklaying skills, you might choose this as a more permanent option. Otherwise, reclaimed timber, or wood from a certified sustainable source, might be the way forward.

Want to sleep(er) on the job?

Pieces of timber, typically cut to 1.2m or 2.4m long, by 150mm high and 100mm wide, are widely available and sold as sleepers on account of their resemblance to the wooden blocks under train tracks. Pine is cheaper than oak or other hardwoods but won't last as long. Kiln-dried wood is less likely to crack and warp as it dries out, than timber that hasn't been seasoned this way, but again this comes at a higher price. You might choose wood that's been treated against rotting, in which case

check that the substances used are considered safe for people and any other life likely to come into contact with your raised bed.

Ensure that the surface you're building on is firm, level and flat. You might even lay down hardcore, old paving slabs or bricks as a foundation, which also prevents contact with damp earth underneath, but this isn't essential. You might choose to line inside the walls of your raised bed with reclaimed, heavy-duty polythene. Separating soil from timber will help delay rotting and will stop any preservatives from leaching into your raised bed.

You can make a square raised bed with four sleepers of the same length in each layer, or a rectangle – two of each of the standard lengths, for example. If you need a different size, ask your supplier to cut them to length for you – their power tools will do the job more easily than you can with a hand saw. You'll still need an electric drill (if you don't have one, maybe you can borrow from a friend, neighbour or local library of things) and a drill bit at least as long as your screws.

Lay the sleepers so that the end of each butts up at right angles against the side of another at the corner. You can build a one-layer bed but might prefer two or three to allow deeper roots and less bending down. When adding layers, overlap the butt joints to make a stronger structure.

At each corner, drill two holes through the side of each sleeper and into the end of the one butting up against it. Fix the pieces together with long timber screws/bolts, about twice as long as the thickness of the sleepers.

Alternatively, you can use square stakes inside each corner, and perhaps also hallway along each side. Hammer each stake at least nine inches into the ground, drill two holes through into each sleeper and attach using two, long, timber screws.

Less durable than sleepers, but much easier to handle, are scaffolding planks. You can use them to make a raised bed in a similar way to sleepers, fixing the planks together using square stakes inside the corners. Try asking a local builder or builders' merchant if they have any old ones they'd sell cheaply to you or (especially if you're running a school or community project) give you.

Making tracks

Retired wooden railway sleepers have long been popular for gardening projects. They are typically made from extremely durable hardwoods, though sometimes the original sources were environmentally and ethically unsound. Repurposing is

great but many were treated with creosote, which is hazardous to people and other creatures and can leach into the soil and waterways. Only buy used sleepers from a trustworthy supplier who can guarantee they were treated with a safer preservative or (better still, as what is considered 'safe' can change over time) are untreated.

Soil preparation

When doing any work on your wheat plot, we recommend the use of protective clothing and equipment, such as strong boots, gloves and overalls or old clothes that you don't mind getting dirty.

As you're working with such a small area, digging out the weeds is easy enough to do. You can then dig through with a spade or fork to remove any large stones or rubble and break up any large lumps of soil. You might want to add some well-rotted manure or garden compost and dig it through to incorporate well. If using a long-straw heritage variety of wheat, though, you probably should avoid fertilising the soil as it can result in fast-growing, weaker stalks, increasing the risk of falling over.

Raised beds and planters

Although waterlogging is unlikely, a layer of rubble or gravel at the bottom can help with drainage. Fill the planter or pot with a mixture of good-quality topsoil and well-rotted manure or garden compost – unless growing a long-straw wheat. As potting compost is very light, growing wheat in a planter full of it on its own isn't recommended as it doesn't offer good root anchorage, and it can dry out easily.

Sowing

The three main options for sowing are dibbing, drilling and broadcasting, described in more detail below. For a small plot, dibbing or drilling will increase your chances of a good crop, but neither is very practical for a larger plot, unless you have some sort of drilling machine or device.

Checking germination

If you have any doubts about the fertility of your wheat seeds, it's a good idea to do a chitting (sprouting) test. This shouldn't be necessary if you got them from a trustworthy source, unless you have stored them for a long time. Even if you're confident the seeds are in good condition, this can be an interesting experiment.

1. Soak a small amount of wheat seeds in water overnight.
2. Clean a jar or other container and pierce holes in its lid.
3. Drain the soaked seeds, place them in the container and put the lid on.
4. Place the jar in a warm position, such as near (but not on) a radiator.
5. Each day, refill the jar with water, swill around, drain and then replace the lid.
6. After three days, count how many seeds have germinated. Your chances of a successful crop will be much better if your germination rate is over 75%.

If doing this as an experiment, your young cereal scientist(s) should keep a daily observation diary, noting (and perhaps drawing) the changes they notice and measure.

Dibbing

Before seed drilling equipment was developed (see below), farmers would use a dibber (basically a pointy stick) to make holes in the ground, with someone walking behind to place seeds in each hole. Today, the use of dibbing in the UK is mainly limited to non-commercial growing of vegetables, fruit and flowers and other garden plants.

Equipment

- Wheat: around 20-30 seeds per linear metre.
- Garden fork and/or spade.
- Rake.
- String.
- Short sticks.
- Ruler or tape measure.
- Dibber: you can buy one or make your own by cutting a piece of dowel (about 2cm in diameter) or old broom handle about 15cm long. You can whittle one end to a blunt point, but this isn't essential.

Method

Soaking the seeds overnight before sowing can help with germination but isn't really necessary unless the ground is very dry.

- Prepare the soil – see above.
- Measure rows about 15cm apart, marking each row with a short stick at each end, connected with string; or perhaps with light-coloured sand.
- Dib each row with holes about 4cm deep and around 15cm apart for spring wheat and 25cm for winter wheat, which is more likely to produce tillers – side shoots.
- Drop two to four seeds into each. A traditional sowers' rhyme goes: 'One for the rook, one for the crow, one will wither and one will grow.'

- Remove the string and gently rake over the plot to fill in each hole without disturbing the seeds.
- Water the plot.

Drilling

This is the most common method of sowing used on UK farms. Seed drills were used in ancient civilisations, for example in China and Sumer. The invention of the modern seed drill is credited to Jethro Tull (the agronomist, rather than the flautist-fronted prog-rock band) in 1701. Drilling can be done manually by hoeing a furrow, dropping seeds into it at roughly even intervals and then raking over.

Equipment needed

- Wheat: Between about 15g and 30g of seed per square metre, or per three linear metres.
- Scales.
- Garden fork and/or spade.
- Hoe, suitable for making a furrow about 4cm deep.
- Rake.
- Ruler or tape measure.
- Cup or other small container.
- Pieces of card, folded in half.
- String.
- Sticks.

* This depends on the fertility of your seeds and time of sowing. The less fertile the seeds and/or later in the season you sow them, the more you're likely to need for a good crop. In the experience of Andrew Forbes of The Brockwell Bake Association, the amount of winter wheat you need might only be 15g in September to 30g in December. It also depends on the sowers. When working with schoolchildren, Cassie Liversidge of Grow Your Own Playground has found that more wheat is often needed.

Method

- Prepare the soil – see above.
- Mark out rows with sticks and string, ideally about 30cm apart. If you have less space, then 15-20cm (enough to get a hoe between rows) will be fine.
- Use the hoe to make a furrow (channel) about 4cm deep along each row.
- Divide the weight according to how many rows you'll be planting. Weigh each portion of the seeds into a small container.

- Walk along each furrow, sprinkling the wheat as you go. Using pieces of card, folded down the middle, can help to channel the seeds into the furrow at a more even rate.
- Remove the string and gently rake over each plot to fill in the furrows without disturbing the seeds.
- Water the plot.

If only planting one square metre, you might just want to divide the wheat into three roughly equal piles, one for each of the rows. Children (and adults, for that matter) might find it easier to sow using a piece of folded card to channel the seeds into the furrow.

Broadcasting

If your plot is more than a few square metres, you might choose the oldest method of sowing wheat, which is simply walking over a prepared field, throwing out seed as you go. This might sound easy but distributing them evenly is a skilled job. It's a quicker way to cover a large area but it's inefficient as the seeds lie on the top of the soil, so many will be lost to birds or won't germinate. Broadcasting seeds also results in a higgledy-piggledy crop, making it much harder to remove weeds than from between the neat rows created by dibbing or drilling.

Equipment needed

- Wheat: about 30-50g of seed per square metre.
- Scales.
- Garden fork and/or spade.
- Rake.

Method

- Prepare the soil – see above.
- Rake over the plot to break up larger lumps of soil and make the surface as smooth as possible. If you have large lumps or big dips, seeds will collect in places and leave bare patches in others.
- Walk forward in as straight a line as possible, gently casting out a handful of seed evenly in an arc about a metre wide from left to right, or right to left, with each stride.
- At the edge of the field/plot, turn, move along about a metre and walk back, repeating step 2 as you go.
- Ideally, you should gently rake the soil to cover the seeds, but this might not be practical on a larger plot.

If you plan to sow a large plot every year, you might want to try to get your hands on an antique seed fiddle (try an online marketplace), which broadcasts seed more evenly, and with less effort, than throwing it.

Caring for your crop

The law of so-and-so states that while weeds look after themselves, the plants you actually want to grow tend to need a bit of TLC to thrive.

Watering

As annual rainfall is usually sufficient in the UK, wheat fields aren't routinely watered. Irrigation during the summer can interfere with wheat maturing and the dampness may also encourage disease. That said, if you are growing it in a pot/planter or shallow raised bed, watering during a dry spring might help the wheat to become established. In these cases, you might also need to water during a dry spring and early summer. A watering can should do the trick.

Weed control

Some weeds, such as broad-leafed docks and tall nettles, will compete with your wheat for light and nutrients, so need to be kept in check. It's easy enough to pull them out of a small plot, though it's better to dig out deep-rooted plants, such as thistles and dandelions, so that nothing's left to regrow. On a larger plot, weeding with a hoe might save you some backache. Dibbing or drilling in neat rows allows you to hoe out weeds between your wheat plants more easily.

'Weeds' are just plants where you don't want them. In the 'right' place, some can be of benefit to growers. On a larger plot you might choose to plant clover, trefoils, vetches, field peas or beans as they can:

- help to suppress competitive weeds.
- act as natural fertiliser factories by absorbing nitrogen from the air and 'fixing' in the soil.
- release nutrients as they die and decompose, helping to improve the health of your soil.
- provide habitat for insects and other wildlife, which not only helps to improve biodiversity but may also be of direct benefit to you – ladybirds and spiders eat nuisance insects and bugs (including greenfly, whitefly and blackfly) for example.

Places you can find information and advice on organic weed control include the websites of the Royal Horticultural Society and, for larger scale growing, Garden Organic, The Organic Research Centre and the US-based National Center for Appropriate Technology.

Diseases

Farmers treat their crops for diseases. Growing at a small scale you might be able to remove affected plants, though diseases tend to affect large sections of the crop all at once. The risk of disease is reduced if you're sowing seed from a certified source on well-drained land that hasn't been used for growing wheat the previous year. Genetic diversity of mixed populations can also help.

Lodging

This is a word for plants falling over. It's usually the result of some combination of strong wind and/or rain, weak straw and loose anchoring in the ground. Lodged wheat stalks dry much more slowly than vertical ones, making them more susceptible to fungal and other diseases, as well as to rodents, pigeons and other hungry creatures. Lodged wheat is also harder to harvest and if ripe grains actually touch the ground, they might start to sprout and so won't be suitable for milling. Older varieties of wheat tend to have longer roots and their ears of ripe wheat tend to be lighter than those of modern varieties, but they're still prone to lodging. Reducing the risk of lodging is one of the reasons cereal breeders developed 'dwarfed' wheat varieties with much shorter stalks.

There's not much you can do to prevent lodging, though avoiding fertilising older varieties will reduce the risk of them growing too tall too quickly (which can result in weaker straw) and growing in a plot sheltered from the wind can help. If wheat lodges while it's still green, it may well right itself. Once the stems are yellow, they won't. As you're only growing a small crop, you can hammer stakes into the ground around your plot and tie rope or cord around at a height of two-thirds or more up the wheat stalks to keep the ears off the ground.

Mill

Although bread can, theoretically, be made from intact, whole grains, they are usually ground into flour using some sort of mill.

Again, there is probably much more here than you need to know. In short, you chop the wheat plants down, leave them somewhere to dry, shake the grains free, get rid of unwanted bits, then grind the wheat into flour.

Harvesting

Most grain grown in the UK is gathered by combine harvesters, so called because they combine the tasks of cutting the stalks, threshing, winnowing and collecting the grains.

Historically, these tasks would have been separate, mainly carried out by people with hand tools, with some machine and animal assistance. As you probably don't have access to a combine harvester, and your crop is too small for one anyway, traditional methods (or approximations of them) are more appropriate.

Health and safety time again: supervise children (and anyone else who needs an eye keeping on them) at all times for all of the activities in this chapter. Whatever you use to harvest your wheat, it will be sharp; during threshing, hard little grains can fly off in all directions - including towards eyes; and wheat husks can blow off to places they're not wanted. As well as old outdoor clothing, it's advisable to wear protective gear, such as goggles, gardening gloves and boots or other sturdy footwear.

Knowing when to harvest

Whether you plant your wheat in the winter or spring, it should be ready to harvest sometime between late July and early September. Farmers use a variety of equipment and tests to know when their wheat is ready, with just the right amount of moisture and protein at the peak of its bread-making potential.

Without all that kit, you'll need to rely on your senses. In simple terms, when the stalks and ears have all turned from green to a golden or a dusty, pale brown colour, it's probably time to gather them in. A traditional way to be more certain if your wheat is ready to harvest is to take an ear, roll it between your hands to free the

berries and then try to split one open by squeezing it between your thumbnail and forefinger. If white goop squidges out, it's still unripe. Once the wheat is ready to harvest, you'll find it hard to split at all. Ideally you should test berries from several plants in a field to get an average result. Try to avoid harvesting in the rain, or if your wheat is wet, as this can cause problems during milling or storage.

Cutting

Garden shears or strong scissors (even the blunt ones schools tend to have) can be used to harvest a small plot. Again, be very careful when using sharp tools and closely supervise all children and any adults who need it.

Take hold of a bundle of stalks with one hand and then cut them close to the ground. Place the bundle aside and move onto the next small section, trying to cut the stalks at roughly the same height. Gathering your small bundles into a sheaf, with the ears together, will make threshing easier.

Your choice of tools might also include a sickle or a scythe, both of which have been used since ancient times for harvesting. The sickle has a crescent-shaped blade and short handle, so is used bending down, while a scythe has a less-curved blade and a longer handle, so is used standing upright. The best sickles for wheat harvesting have a serrated blade, which will saw through tough straw with more ease. When harvesting wheat with a scythe, a grain cradle is needed to stop the cut straw falling higgledy-piggledy, which would make sheaving very difficult. Using either of these hazardous agricultural tools is best left to experts. If you're considering using one, you really should try to find an expert willing to lead your harvesting session safely, or just to give a demonstration before you dig out those blunt scissors.

Drying

For farmers, getting the moisture level of wheat and other cereals right is a balancing act. If the moisture content of the grain is too high, it will be much more susceptible to spoilage during storage. This can have a negative effect on breadmaking quality (therefore financial value) and may even make it unusable. On the other hand, grain is bought and sold by weight and the energy cost of hot air dryers is high, so overuse literally causes a farmer's profit to evaporate. A high moisture content can cause difficulty when milling as well. If you have access to a moisture metre, you should aim for 13-15% but don't worry if you don't for a small-scale growing project.

Sheaves and stooking

A traditional way of drying wheat is gathering and bundling the stalks (with the ears still attached) into sheaves, which are then collected together and stacked upright into stooks in the field and left to dry for days or even weeks. The dried stooks would then be gathered together in the field and made into even larger creations (with names such as mows, ricks and thatched stacks) or taken into a barn. Although you're probably not going to store your grain for long, if at all, you might want to have a go anyway.

Making a sheaf

- Take five or six whole wheat stalks and twist them together to form a sort of rope. If your stalks aren't long enough, you can use string or twine instead.
- If you have harvested more than a handful of wheat, make a sheaf by gathering together a bundle as large as you can manage comfortably in your arms, with the cut ends all together and roughly level with each other.
- Wind the 'rope' around the middle of the bundle, ideally twice, and tuck the loose end under itself to stop it coming undone. Alternatively, wrap it round once, twist the two ends across each other, leaving one end much longer and tuck this end into the middle of the bundled wheat.

Making a stook

If you have a large enough harvest to make a number of sheaves, you can build them into a stook.

- Take a sheaf, tap the cut end to the ground at a slight angle to key it in with the stubble.
- Take a second sheaf, tap it into the ground opposite the first one a short distance away.
- Lean the two sheaves towards each other and gently shuffle the heads against each other to lock the two together and prevent them from blowing over.
- If you have more sheaves, make them into another stook right next to the first, brushing the two together for increased stability.
- An alternative method is to take at least five sheaves, arranged in a circular or rectangular formation, ideally with an additional sheaf on top to act as a 'roof'.

As you've only grown a small amount of wheat, you might prefer to take your sheaves somewhere under cover (perhaps in a shed, or inside the school - if that's where you're growing) to dry, so they don't get soggy if it rains. If you can't bring your wheat inside, then securing a tarpaulin or plastic sheet over it will help to keep

it dry. Wherever the wheat is, air needs to be able to circulate around the stalks/sheaves and ideally the place should be rodent-proof – you might find that hanging the wheat from a rafter/roof (careful on that ladder!) is the answer.

Threshing

Before you can mill your wheat, you need to remove it from the stalks and get rid of the other inedible bits, the first stage of which is threshing (or thrashing) to free the grain.

As with the activities in the growing section, we strongly recommend you use protective gear. Goggles will protect eyes from flying wheat and other bits, a facemask will help reduce dust reaching lungs, and overalls or old clothes will keep your party frock clean.

One way to thresh is to choose a clean, hard, dry surface or object that won't be damaged when you smash a bundle of wheat against it – like a wall, floor or empty dustbin.

- Lay down a large piece of tarpaulin, plastic sheeting, old blanket, or similar to collect the grain.
- Hold a bundle of wheat tightly with two hands, close to the cut end.
- Bash the grain end against the hard object.
- Repeat until all of the grains have come free.
- Take another bundle and repeat the process.
- Hold the sheet by all four corners (it might require several people), gather together, and then tip the grain into a container.

Alternatively, you could put your bundle of wheat into a hessian sack or an old, unwanted pillowcase, ears first; gather the open end around the stalks tightly; then smack the sack or pillowcase against your hard object or surface. Other options include thrashing each bundle around inside a clean, dry dustbin; and lying the stalks down, then walking over the heads.

Winnowing

The next stage is blowing away the remaining chaff (bits of husk, stalk and so on), leaving the heavier grain behind for collection. This can be done outside in a light breeze by throwing the grain up in the air (perhaps using a shallow tray or basket) or dropping it down from as high as you can manage (careful if standing on a stepladder, desk, chair etc.), onto a large sheet or cleaned floor below.

Another option is dropping the grain into a large bucket, washing up bowl or bin, with a desktop or room fan, hair dryer, or vacuum cleaner with a reverse setting, positioned towards the falling grain. A third way is to simply lay the grain out on a sheet and fan the chaff away with a large piece of stiff card.

Sieving

Using a grain sieve will help to remove heavier pieces of stalk, ears of wheat that didn't break up, stones and other unwanted bits. Ideally, you should then use a second sieve with a finer mesh that will allow unwanted small seeds and debris to fall through but retain your wheat. Have a look online but don't worry if you can't get hold of these as you can remove the unwanted bits and bobs from a small batch of wheat by hand.

Checking and storing

You'll probably use the golden goodness you've grown more or less straight away. To be sure that something else doesn't chow down on your wheat before you get a chance, though, you need to store it somewhere that's cool, dry and rodent/insect proof. Depending on how much you've produced, a jar or other container with a lid should do the trick. Before you store your wheat, check it's bone dry and pick out any:

- weevils or other creepy crawlies.
- black pellets – they might well be rodent poo.

Sadly, if you find any of the following, you'll need to throw away the whole batch of wheat:

- grains that are mouldy or have a powdery coating.
- elongated grains that are purple or black. This means it's infected by a fungus called ergot, which is toxic.
- small, round black balls, which burst and release black or brown powder that smells like bad fish. This is a fungal infection known as smut or bunt. Though not poisonous, it will spoil the taste of your flour and the spores will infect other grains.

Milling

Unless you want to get very old-school (as in prehistoric) by bashing your grain between two rocks or in a pestle and mortar, you'll need some sort of mill to make it into flour. When milling, try to feed the grain in a steady, constant stream. Feel the

flour as it's produced and if it's anything more than slightly warm, then you'll need to slow the mill down or stop for a while to allow the mill to cool.

Quern

The saddle quern is the oldest form of this type of milling device. A roughly cylindrical stone (the handstone) is pushed and pulled back and forth to grind the grain against a flattish, roughly rectangular stone. The oldest known in the UK date back to perhaps around 4000BCE but older examples have been found in countries including Egypt, Mexico (where it's called a metate) and China.

The rotary quern, which is thought to have reached England in around 400BCE, is more efficient than the saddle quern. It is made of two parts: a static lower stone and a mobile upper one. The lower stone might be conical or dome-shaped and the upper one hollowed out to fit it. The top stone has one or two handles to turn it and a hole in the middle, through which grain is poured. As the upper stone is turned and the grain is ground, the flour comes out all around the edge of the gap between the upper and lower stone, which in some cases has a channel around it to collect the flour.

Small stone mills

Traditional wind- and water-powered flour mills in the UK were usually based around a pair of flat, circular millstones, typically made from a hard rock, such as granite, chert (a type of quartz), marble or a suitable type of sandstone or limestone. The bedstone is fixed in place, with the runner stone rotating a tiny, adjustable distance above it, or beside it if the stones are set vertically. Each stone has channels carved into it to help grind the grain and direct the flour outwards. To collect the flour, there might be a channel around the bedstone, a hopper beneath it, or a spout to the side. You can read more about traditional mills on pages 91 to 96.

Pairs of millstones are still available in different sizes – an internet search will help you find something suitable. They range from a few inches to a couple of feet in diameter. The distance between the stones can be adjusted in some mills to produce coarser or finer flours. Some are hand-turned or can be adapted to be driven by an alternative power source, such as a static bicycle. Others are built into a tabletop mill with an electric motor or a handle to turn the runner stone manually.

Plate mill

In this type of mill, a grooved steel plate revolves very close to another, static, grooved steel plate. These are usually vertical and grain is fed in through a hopper at the top. Power is provided by a manually cranked handle or can be run by an engine or motor in some models. Plate mills used to be common on farms, so it might be possible to find one at a farm auction, antique shop or by an online search, though they tend to produce a coarse meal, rather than fine flour.

Other options

An electric, or hand-cranked, coffee grinder on its finest setting can be used to turn grain into flour. Some will only produce very coarse flour and it's a relatively time-consuming way of milling any more than a very small amount, though. Another option is to use food processor or a jug-type blender, though again the results might not be ideal.

A local traditional mill

If you know of a working wind or watermill locally, get in touch to see if they might be able to help with your Bake Your Lawn project, particularly if you're running it with a school or community group. If you're not sure if there's one round your way, have a look at the websites of the Traditional Cornmillers Guild, the Mills Section of the Society for the Protection of Ancient Buildings, the National Trust, or the Britain and Ireland Community Grains Association.

Many traditional mills welcome visitors all year round, but some have set open days and others ask that you make an appointment first. A few (but growing number of) Real Bread bakeries and cereal farmers also have their own small mills. Unless it has educational facilities, it's unlikely that a modern roller mill will be able to help you mill your grain.

If considering taking your wheat along to a mill, please make contact ahead of your visit to ask the miller, mill owner or custodian if they might be able to help mill your wheat. Note that even if your wheat looks in good condition, a miller might inspect it and say otherwise. There may be other reasons that it turns out they are unable to mill your grain – a certified organic mill can only accept grain that's been grown on a certified organic farm, for example.

Bolting

The wholemeal flour you have produced contains all of the grain and so is also known as 100% extraction flour. This makes delicious, nutritious Real Bread and ensures that all the energy that you (and nature) have put into it goes to good use feeding people.

You might want to produce a lighter flour, though. To do this, you will need to remove the larger particles of bran and germ, which can be done by sieving it – also known as bolting. Historically, the finest bolting cloth was made from silk but it's now usually made from steel or a synthetic fibre. Drum-shaped flour sieves are available for bolting by hand. The combination of a 650 micron to 1,000 micron mesh (to remove larger bran flakes) and a 375 micron one will produce a light brown flour. If the mill you use enables you to do so, you can re-mill the meal that gets caught by the finer sieve, then bolt it again.

Modern milling

The roller milling process is ruthlessly efficient at stripping the bran and germ away from the endosperm. The streams then have to be recombined in different combinations and proportions to produce particular types of flour.

By contrast, even if stoneground flour is passed through the finest sieve or bolting cloth, miniscule particles of all parts of the grain will remain. This gives bolted stoneground flour a creamy, beige or even brown colour, as well as a wheatier flavour and aroma than roller miller flour. Read more in the Lessons in Loaf section on pages 97 and 98.

Maturing

Flour is at its nutritional peak just after milling, before oxidation and other processes start to affect the levels of enzyme activity, vitamins and other micronutrients. On the other hand, oxidation results in aged or matured flour producing stronger gluten than fresh (also known as 'green') flour. If you want to leave your flour for two or three weeks before baking, go for it. Otherwise, you can make great bread with it straight from the mill. You might find that fresh flour absorbs more water and that you get better results using the stretch and fold technique (see pages 46 and 47) to build up gluten strength. Past a certain point, flour will start to become stale and may develop undesirable flavours. Wholemeal flour is more prone to this as it contains higher levels of oil, which oxidise and eventually become rancid.

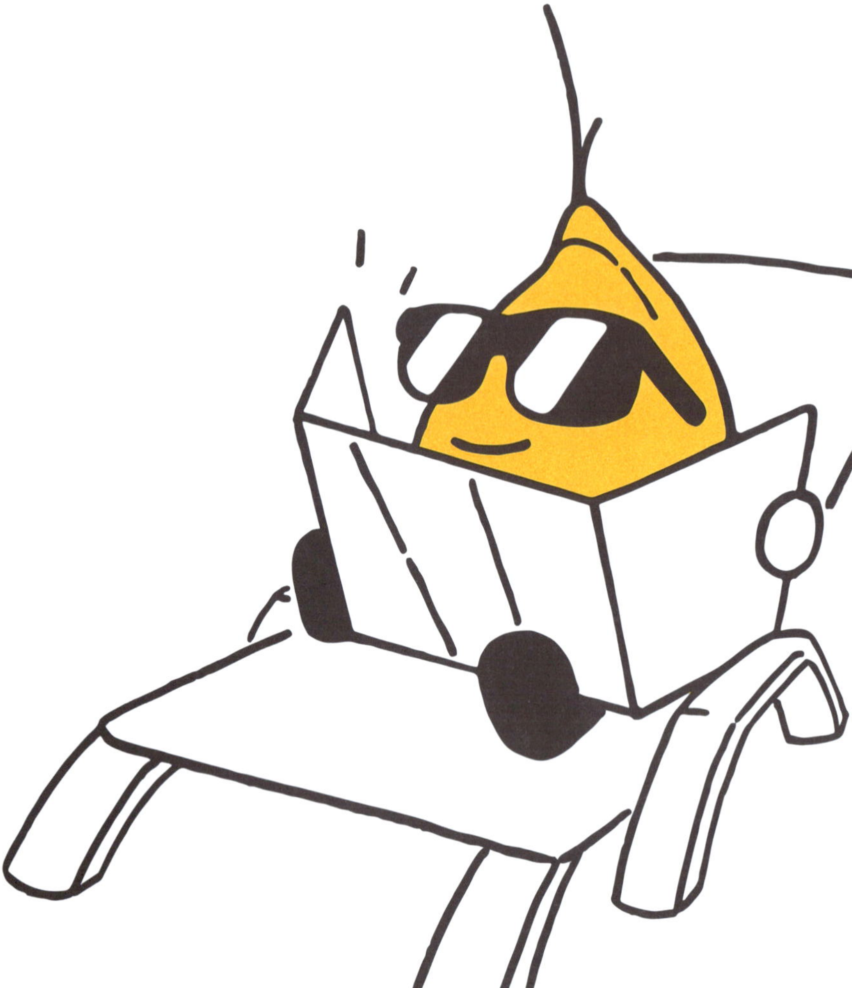

Bake

You've grown your own flour! How great does that feel? Now, let's make Real Bread with it.

The process is basically: measure, mix, wait, shape and bake. Even if it goes 'wrong' (which often just means 'different to how I planned it') you'll almost certainly end up with something that tastes great. You can then dust yourself off and have another go.

Ingredients

You can turn your flour into Real Bread using as few as one or two more natural ingredients.

Water

This is the second main ingredient of bread after flour. It is essential to the process of wheat proteins combining to form gluten and hydrating starch, another key building block of dough. Water also enables other ingredients to dissolve or disperse through the dough and produces steam that helps it to rise.

Don't be shy of using more water than you think is enough. As Real Bread Campaign co-founder Andrew Whitley says: 'the wetter the better.' If the dough sticks to your hands, you can clean them using a dough scraper, then rub them with dry flour. Using less water (or adding more flour) than a recipe says can result in bread that's tight, dry and dense.

As many artisan and home bakers do, you can make great bread using tap water. If you're thinking of using bottled water for baking, don't bother as it's a waste of energy, natural resources and your money. The authors of the book Modernist Bread experimented with water treated five different ways and reported almost no difference in the taste or size of the loaves.

Hydration

Professional bakers sometimes refer to the amount of water used relative to the flour as hydration. A dough with equal weights of flour and water is 100% hydration and one with half as much water as flour is 50% hydration. Dough for a tin loaf might be around 65% hydration, while focaccia dough may be between 80% to 90% hydration or even higher.

Salt

Technically, you can make bread without any salt (as some breads, including pane Toscano, illustrate) but a little bit helps to boost the flavour. It also has an effect on browning and gluten strength, but that's beyond the scope of this book.

Despite what you might've read or heard, one form of common salt (sodium chloride) isn't more or less healthy, tasty or salty than another, though you might want to avoid brands with anti-caking agents added. You might also prefer to use salt from a smaller, independent producer.

Salt and health

While a small amount of salt is necessary for a number of processes in the human body, the general consensus is that too much can be bad for our health. Excess salt has been linked to high blood pressure, which can contribute to an increased risk of conditions including heart disease and stroke. We follow the UK government's salt reduction target, which in 2020 was set at a maximum of 1g of salt per 100g of baked bread. Though hydration and other ingredients will have an effect on percentages, as a rough guideline, try not to use more than 6g (about a level teaspoon) of salt per 500g of flour.

Yeast

You can make unleavened flatbread from just flour, water and salt, or nurture the yeasts and bacteria naturally present in that flour to create a starter culture to make sourdough bread. As many Real Bread makers do, though, you might prefer to use baker's yeast to make your dough rise.

Yeasts are microscopic, single-celled fungi. The species of yeast usually used in breadmaking is *Saccharomyces cerevisiae*, commonly known as baker's (and brewer's) yeast. Yeast cells produce enzymes that convert some of the starch in flour into sugars on which they feed, then give off carbon dioxide as a by-product of respiration. This gas is the main thing that makes dough rise.

Most bread and industrial loaf products are made to rise using baker's yeast that has been cultured/grown in a factory. The process of culturing and isolating single strains of yeast was developed in the mid to late 1800s and refined to more or less the current process by the 1920s. The yeast cells are grown in a nutrient solution (often molasses, a by-product of refining sugar) which is then rinsed away. The yeast cells are separated from the liquid by centrifugal force and then compressed into blocks or dried as small pellets or granules.

Many recipes from the mid-20th century onwards tend to call for amounts of yeast (and proving temperatures) high enough to speed up the dough to be ready to bake in under an hour. It's possible to slow things down by using less yeast and cooler temperatures. This can help improve the flavour and texture of your bread, and it's also good for people who don't like their bread to smell and taste of yeast. Many recipes tell you to mix yeast with warm water (and maybe sugar as well) and leave it to see if it bubbles before using, though this test isn't necessary unless you have doubts about its freshness.

If you choose to work with baker's yeast, always read the ingredients list. Almost every brand of dried active and fast acting yeast we've seen in the UK contains one or more additives, which have no place in Real Bread.

Forms of yeast

Baker's yeast is available in several forms:

Fresh

It is sold as beige, fudge-like blocks. Fresh yeast is used by many small bakeries and some home bakers, though it's not always easy to find in the UK. It needs to be kept refrigerated and still has a relatively short shelf-life – perhaps two to three weeks. It can be wrapped and frozen, though results reported by bakers vary. To ensure fresh yeast gets distributed evenly in your dough, you can either rub it into some of the flour, or disperse it in some of the water, before mixing with the rest of the ingredients.

Dried active

This is same as fresh yeast but has been dehydrated to remove most of the moisture. It is sold in packs of small, spherical pellets. It can be stored for years before the packaging's vacuum seal is broken and months afterwards, as long as it's kept cool and dry. This also needs to be dispersed in some of the water from the recipe before adding to the rest of the ingredients.

Fast acting

Also known as quick, instant, quick or easy bake yeast. The granules are much finer than dried active yeast, so fast-acting yeast can be mixed straight in with the other ingredients.

Other ingredients

Though many recipes might lead you to believe otherwise, you don't need to add any sort of sugar or fat/oil when making plain bread. That's not to say you shouldn't use unprocessed or minimally processed ingredients (such as eggs, dairy products, honey, oils, nuts, seeds, herbs, fruit, vegetables etc.) when making an enriched or flavoured bread, though.

Anything made with chemical raising agents (e.g. baking powder/soda and self-raising flour) or other additives (as defined in food law) fall outside the Campaign's definition of Real Bread – see page 7.

Equipment

The only bits of kit you actually need to make Real Bread are something to measure your ingredients; something to mix them in or on; and something hot to cook the dough in or on.

Here are some notes on these and other handy bits and bobs than can help to make the process easier but please don't feel you need to get hold or all of them. If you're running a hands-on, skill-sharing session with a group, don't forget a set of equipment for each person, including yourself.

Aprons

To prevent clothes from getting messy with flour and other ingredients.

Baking parchment / greaseproof paper

Can be used instead of, or as well as, greasing a baking tray. Can also be used to lower dough into a cooking pot, if you're using one. If you're baking with a group, each baker can write their name on the underside of a slip of this paper to help identify whose loaves/rolls are whose after baking.

Baking / pizza stone

Can be used for pizzas and other flatbreads that benefit from a good whack of conducted heat right at the start of baking. Some people report they get better results than with a baking tray, others don't find much if any difference.

Baking tray

Non-stick or uncoated. The thicker the baking tray the better, to help distribute heat evenly.

Blade

To help bread expand fully during baking, and to control where it bursts, professional bakers often use a lame, grignette or super-sharp small knife to score dough immediately before it goes into the oven. Keep this out of the reach of children!

Bread / loaf tin

Always grease/oil the inside of a tin before putting your dough in. If your loaf doesn't come out of the tin easily after baking, leave it a few minutes and then try again – the escaping steam and bread shrinking back can help to loosen it. If it still sticks, slide a thin, flexible plastic spatula (metal can ruin the coating of a tin) or a dough scraper between the bread and tin, being careful not to puncture your loaf.

Casserole dish

Many professional bakers' ovens have steam generators. Baking your bread in a casserole dish, or other thick-walled cooking vessel with a lid, such as a Dutch pot, can help you get similar results as it traps steam generated by the dough in the early stages of baking. See the no-knead recipe of pages 61 and 62.

Cooling rack

Once your bread is baked, if you don't remove it from whatever you bake it in or on, the steam it releases as it cools will condense, causing the bottom to 'sweat' and it can go soggy. Instead, place the bread on something that will allow air to circulate around it, such as a wire cake rack or a shelf from the oven. You can also place a loaf on top of a bread tin, at a right angle to it.

Dough scraper

A plastic scraper is a cheap but oh-so-useful bit of kit. You can use it to mix and cut dough; to lift it out of a bowl or off a work surface; and to scrape any scraps or dried bits off bowls, hands and work surfaces when cleaning up.

Measuring jug

Even if you use scales to weigh your liquids (see note below) a jug can be handy to transfer water from the tap, rather than taking a mixing bowl to the sink. A jug can also be used to for beating eggs or mixing ingredients together before pouring them into the main mixture.

Mixing bowl

Any food-safe bowl or container will do but it's advisable to use one that won't break if/when it gets dropped. It should be large enough for the dough to double in size - one with a three-litre capacity should be okay for up to 1kg of dough. Alternatively, you can tip the dry ingredients onto a clean work surface, make a well in the centre, pour in the liquid and then incorporate the flour etc. working from the outside edge inwards.

Oven

The recipes in this book are suitable for a domestic gas or electric oven. If you have access to a bakery or catering oven (e.g. in a school canteen) you might get even better results. It should go without saying but an oven gets hot, so keep young children away from it and supervise any older children you believe are responsible enough to use one. Always load the dough in and the bread out yourself, standing clear of the blast of steam that escapes as you open the door.

A number of schools and community groups that participated in our original Bake Your Lawn and Lessons in Loaf projects built their own cob/clay ovens. See pages 141 and 142 in the 'find out more' section of books and other sources of information on doing this.

Oven gloves / mitts

To stop getting hands burned. Alternatively, fold a tea towel to at least quadruple thickness. Ensure whatever you use is clean and dry. Hot metal in contact with moisture will turn it to steam, which may scald you.

Peel

A thin, flat, metal or wooden paddle with a handle that can be used for loading pizza or other bread into and out of an oven. Alternatives for use in a domestic oven include a piece of hardboard, stiff cardboard, or a baking sheet without a lip on at least one edge.

Plastic bag

Used to keep dough from drying out and forming a skin whilst proving. Put your bowl of dough inside the bag, making a 'tent' so that the top of the bag doesn't stick to the dough. Do the same with the dough once it's in a tin or on a tray. When you have finished, turn the bag inside out to dry so you can use it again and again. Another option is a shower cap but if you loathe the very existence of plastic bags, even reused ones, you can use a clean, damp tea towel over the bowl. Alternatively you can make and prove dough in a large, food-safe container with a lid.

Proving basket

As an alternative to using a bread tin, you can prove in a special basket (dusted with flour to prevent sticking), then turn the dough out onto a baking tray immediately before putting it in the oven. In the UK, they are also commonly known by their French or German name – bannetons and brotformen. They are usually made of rattan or wood pulp and need to be left to dry after use to prevent mould. Some bakers report success using cheap, plastic bread baskets you see on tables in some eateries.

Scales

For accuracy, we recommend using electronic scales to weigh all ingredients, including liquids. If you don't have access to electronic scales, then accurate conventional scales, a measuring jug and measuring spoons will help you to get more predictable and consistent results.

Stove / hob

Whether or not you have access to an oven, you can use a pan on a hob to make flatbreads or steamed buns. Portable ones are available if making bread away from a kitchen. The safety advice is similar to that for an oven.

Thermometers

As the thermostats in domestic ovens aren't always accurate, an oven thermometer is useful to ensure you're baking at the temperature you want. A baking thermometer can be used to test the internal temperature of bread, which should be about 88-98°C at the centre. If you get really serious about breadmaking, to help predict the proving time more accurately you might use a thermometer to check the temperature of the water you use, and the temperature of the finished dough.

Techniques

Here are a few terms you will see in many bread recipes to help understand why you need (and, in some cases, might not need) to do them.

Kneading

This is a word for working the dough to develop the gluten and so build up the strength of your dough. There is no right or wrong way to knead. Some bakers hold one end of the dough against the work surface with one hand, push the other end away from themselves with the heel of the other hand, bring the dough back together and repeat many times. Others take the dough (particularly if wet and sticky) and flick it forwards so that it stretches out and one end sticks to the work surface. They then fold the end in their hand back to the stuck end, then stretch again, occasionally unsticking the dough with a scraper and starting again.

However you work your dough, try to do so without flour on the work surface. If you do add flour, keep it to an absolute minimum as it will get mixed in with the dough. This can result in a drier dough than planned, which might not rise as well, or even patches of flour inside your bread. Though it might sound odd, if your dough is very wet, you can use water on your hands and work surface to help prevent the dough from sticking – and don't forget that a dough scraper is your friend. The less time your hands are in contact with the dough on each push or pull, the less it should stick to you.

Not kneading

Let time and water do the work! Back in the 20th century, many of us were brought up to believe kneading is an essential part of breadmaking. The reality is that, given enough water and time, gluten will develop even if the dough is left to its own devices. Mechanical action (either by hand or in a mixer) simply speeds the process up. The origins of no-knead breadmaking are lost in time. In recent decades, the technique was re-popularised in the USA and beyond by Suzanne Dunaway's 1999 book No Need to Knead, and later by the baker Jim Lahey and food writer Mark Bittman in a New York Times article. We've included a no-knead recipe on pages 61 and 62.

Stretch and fold

If you are proving dough over a number of hours and able to return to it every 10-60 minutes during that time, this method can be used to reduce or replace the kneading you do to develop gluten. Take an edge of the dough, lift and stretch it over to the other side. Now take the opposite edge and repeat, folding it over to where you began the first stretch. Repeat this with the edges of the dough at right angles to the first two. Leave the dough to rest for at least 10 minutes and repeat the four stretches and folds.

Fermentation rising and proving

As noted in the ingredients section, yeast cells produce an enzyme that breaks down some of the starch in flour into simpler sugars that they can use for energy. A by-product of these processes is the carbon dioxide that makes dough rise. The word that many bakers use for this period of fermentation, during which the dough rises, is proving – some bakers say proofing, which is more common in American English. It is often divided into stages, including the bulk proof of all of the ingredients together, and the final proof of piece of the dough after shaping.

Speeding and slowing fermentation

There are a few ways to control the amount of time dough takes to rise fully, each of which can be used on its own or in combination with other methods. Options for an 'accelerator' include proving at a higher temperature, using more yeast or less salt. 'Brakes' that can be used to slow down the metabolism of the yeast include proving at a lower temperature, using less yeast or more salt.

Being able to control the rate at which dough rises is important in a bakery, so that each batch of loaves is ready at a time that fits into the baking schedule. Bakers used to rely on adjusting salt and yeast levels, as well as water temperature, but this is not always reliable, particularly in extremely hot or cold weather. Sometimes it resulted in very salty bread. For more accurate control, some bakeries now have retarders, which are like large fridges, to slow fermentation and some have provers that keep dough at a higher temperature, to speed up the process.

Dividing and scaling

If you are baking a batch of loves or rolls, or something formed from more than one piece (e.g. a plait) you will need to divide the dough. This is best done with your trusty dough scraper. You can do it by eye but it's better to use scales to check that pieces of dough in a batch are of equal weight. This helps them to bake at the same speed and it looks better to have them identical. For professional bakers it is important (or even legally required) that each product's weight is as advertised.

Shaping

You can just roll dough into a ball, sausage, or whatever shape, but sometimes will find it doesn't come out of the oven quite as you expected.

More experienced bakers shape dough carefully, stretching the outside of it for strength and pinching it together at the meeting point of two parts that have been pulled together. This gives a better chance of avoiding unexpected bursts, or ruptures, that can have a negative impact on the look – and even texture – of your Real Bread. Shaping is easier if the dough is slightly tacky, so try to minimise or avoid dusting it or the work surface with flour, or the dough might skate about and not knit together so easily at the joins.

If you can have a lesson, or otherwise spend some time, with a skilled baker, they will show you their ways of shaping. The second-best option is watching video clips online to see various techniques different bakers use. Though it's hard to describe shaping in print, here we go for two basic shapes…

Ball

Press the dough out into a roughly square shape. Fold each of the four corners into the centre of the square and press down. Next, fold the corners of the new square you've created to the new centre and press them down again.

Turn the dough over so that the seam-side (i.e. the messy bit) is underneath. Starting with your hands together, palms down, rest them lightly on top of the dough and slide them down round it. Keep contact with the dough to pull it down and round, creating tension in its outer surface. Your hands will meet palm-side up underneath the dough, pinching it together between the little finger side of your hands.

Move your hands back to the start position, giving the dough a quarter turn clockwise as you go, then repeat the previous step. You'll need to do this a few times until you can feel tightness in the dough. Finish by pinching the underside of the dough to ensure the loose bits have knitted together.

Another method for small pieces of dough that fit into one hand (buns, for example) is to cup your hand lightly on top of the dough and roll it in small circles against the work surface. Between roughly the 12 o'clock and six o'clock positions of each circle, apply slight pressure to the dough with the little finger side of your hand to create tension. You can also do this against the palm of your other hand, rather than the work surface. Finish by pinching the underside of the dough to ensure the loose bits have knitted together.

Baton or sausage shape

Press the dough out into a roughly square shape. Fold each of the four corners into the centre of the square and press down. Next, fold the corners of the new square you've created to the new centre and press them down again.

Keeping the seam (messy) side of the dough up, put your hands together with the tips of your longest fingers touching, at the far edge of the dough. Roll the whole width of the dough about a third of the way towards you. Use the little finger sides of your hands to press the edge down to where it meets the rest of the dough. Move your hands back to the start position and repeat the previous steps, creating tension on the outside of the dough as you pull it a further third towards you. Once you have down this a third time, pinch the seam closed and roll the dough back and forth a couple of times to even it out.

Flatbreads

If you can get your hands on a tortilla, roti/chapati or other flatbread press, give it a go. Roll dough into a small ball (check the press's instructions or the Internet for a guide on size/weight), with a sheet of baking parchment / greaseproof paper underneath and another on top of the dough, place it in the centre of the press and then push the lever down smoothly and firmly. You might need to rotate the dough by 90° and repeat.

Otherwise, it's time to bring out the rolling pin and ignore the 'don't add too much extra flour' advice above. Roll dough into a small ball in your hands, then dust the worksurface and top of the dough with flour. Gently press the dough flat with one hand. Starting right at the edge (rather than halfway across) the dough, roll the pin all the way across the dough, then roll it all the way back again. Try to apply even pressure with each hand, either at each end of the pin (if it has handles) or with your fingers and palms spaced an even distance from the centre and ends of a pin without a handle. Repeat the dust, roll and rotate process until the dough is a circle (more or less) about 2mm thick. Other flatbreads (pita, for example) call for different thicknesses, so go with what the recipe says. Some people pride themselves in getting a near-perfect circle, without raggedy edges, but please don't obsess over this – especially when working with junior bakers.

Animals and more

Especially if baking with younger children, making dough into different shapes can be a way of adding fun and creativity, helping to make the session more engaging and memorable. We've seen snakes, hedgehogs, teddy bears, human figures, favourite characters and more. Try to guide the budding baker(s) in making different sections of the dough fairly similar in size/thickness to avoid part being underbaked and/or burnt.

Heating the oven

Real Bread needs to be baked in an oven that's already up to the temperature stated in the recipe. You will not get good results if you load dough into a cooler oven. To give your dough the best chance of shining, it needs a good wallop of heat straight away directly from the floor/sole of the oven, by convection from rising hot air and radiating from the oven walls.

Finger poke test

When is dough fully proved and ready to bake? This is another question that's hard to answer in print. Even if you've been precise with every measurement of ingredients, temperature and so on, it's not always possible to say dough needs to prove for exactly X minutes or hours. The actual answer is 'when it's ready', which is not very useful, is it? Sorry.

Something you can use as a guide is pressing the dough gently with a finger or the pad at the base of your thumb. If the dough springs back quickly, it's not ready; if it collapses totally, you've probably left it too long. What you want to see is the dough slowly returning to shape and erasing the dent you have made. It's one of those things that you learn through experience and perhaps making bread with an experienced, skilled baker who can say: "here, give this dough a poke. That's what it feels like when it's ready to bake."

Scoring

The internet is awash with photos and videos that might make you think that scoring dough is purely artistic, rather than functional. At one time, however, it helped to distinguish between loaves – particularly handy if baking in communal ovens or making more than one type of bread at a time. Scoring also allows dough to expand more in the early stage of baking, so that the bread is less dense. It also helps to control where the dough expands, reducing the risk of unwanted bursts (splits) in the crust.

Scoring should be done in a swift, decisive stroke with a very sharp blade (see page 43) just before you load dough into the oven. If you do it any earlier, the cut will lose definition or might disappear altogether. You won't get good results using a blunt knife, sawing back and forth, snagging the dough, having multiple attempts, or barely breaking the surface.

How to tell if bread is fully baked

Many professional bakers using temperature probes to check. The general rule is that bread should be about 95°C at the centre. Your other option is the old 'knock on the bottom and if it sounds hollow, it's done' trick. It's another of those things that's virtually impossible to explain in writing and can only be learned from experience and/or spending time with an experienced baker.

Recipes

Though this isn't a recipe book, here are a few to get you going. You can find free recipes on our website and read more about breadmaking in our book **Slow Dough: Real Bread**.

All of the following are written for wholemeal flour but you can replace or some or all of it with white flour. If you do, you might need to reduce the amount of water by 5-10% to account for the reduced amount of the absorbent bran.

Before you start, wipe down all work surfaces and make sure everyone making bread has washed their hands, removed jewellery, tied long hair back, put on aprons and covered any cuts. Children should be supervised at all times and stages of the process that involve heat (using an oven, frying pan or fire, for example) or sharp blade (such as scoring dough or chopping vegetables) should be done by a competent adult.

Basic (but brilliant) bread

This is a simple, versatile Real Bread dough that can be used to make loaves, rolls, flatbreads or in all sorts of other ways. You can adapt it by adding more water or other natural ingredients, such as cheese, seeds, nuts etc. - having first checked for allergies, of course.

Ingredients

Makes one loaf (about 750g) or eight to twelve small rolls.

- 500g wholemeal flour
- 360g hand warm (about 25°C) water. Feel free to use more

- 10g fresh yeast*
- 7g salt
- A little butter or oil for greasing the baking tray

*Or 5g dried active yeast, or about 3.5g fast-acting yeast – if you can find an additive-free brand.

Equipment

- Scales
- Mixing bowl
- Plastic bag (or tea towel)
- Loaf tin or baking tray
- Oven
- Oven gloves
- Cooling rack

Method

1. Mix all of the ingredients together until there are no dry bits left and you have a shaggy dough. If it seems too dry, add a little more water.
2. Pick up the dough and knead until it feels stretchy and silky. This might take about 10 or 15 minutes but see notes on pages 46 and 47. Don't worry that it starts out sticky - it will get less so as you go. Please avoid the temptation to add extra flour.
3. Shape the dough into a ball and place in the bowl. To stop the dough from drying out and forming a 'skin', put the bowl into a plastic bag or cover with a damp towel, making sure that it won't touch the dough. Leave for about 60 minutes to prove. This doesn't need to be anywhere particularly warm, though if the room is very cold, the dough will take longer to rise.
4. Press and fold the dough gently to get rid of any large bubbles, then mould it into the desired shape – see pages 48 and 49. To make a loaf, grease the tin (or baking tray, if making a free-standing loaf), follow the guide for shaping a baton and place the dough seam-side (where the join is) down into / onto it.
5. Cover the dough again and leave to rise for about another 30 to 40 minutes.
6. About 20 minutes before the dough is ready to bake, turn the oven on to heat up to 220°C / gas mark 7.
7. Uncover the dough, making sure the cover doesn't touch the dough (because it will stick, which could lead to the dough collapsing) and slide the tray or tin into the oven.
8. The baking time will be about 15–20 minutes for rolls and 30–40 minutes for a large loaf.

9. Wearing oven gloves, remove the Real Bread from the oven, turn it out onto a wire rack, cover with a clean, dry teatowel and leave to cool before eating or putting into a bag/container. The teatowel traps some of the escaping steam, which helps to keep the bread soft.

Variations on the basic dough

Rather than being radically different, the recipes for many Real Breads around the world are very similar, perhaps varying only in ratios of flour, water, yeast and salt. Other differences are due to omitting an ingredient (perhaps yeast or salt) or adding one – such as oil. The method also has a big influence – a piece of dough will produce a very different bread depending on whether it is baked, steamed or fried.

Here are some changes to the recipe above. As with almost every bread, there is no single 'genuine' recipe for any of them but if you want a version of one that's more 'authentic', look up recipes from people whose culinary cultural heritage includes it and pick one you like. What you end up with will still be different from theirs as everything you use isn't exactly the same – most notably the homegrown flour that is unique to you!

Bagels

Bagels are typically made using a very high-protein, white flour, but you might want to give it a go using your wholemeal. Decrease the water in the recipe to about 325-340g. After the first proof, divide the dough into 8-12 pieces and shape into rings. You can do this by rolling the pieces into balls, making a hole in the middle of each with your fingers, gently stretching it out and then, using two fingers through the hole, rolling it back and forth against the worksurface. Give the ring a small turn after each back and forth until you've rolled all the way round. Another method is to roll each ball into a sausage shape, overlap the ends slightly and roll back and forth in the same way but just at the join.

After the second proof come the bit that distinguishes a bagel from any other bread roll – boiling the dough. This part should be done by a responsible adult, not a child. Once the oven is almost up to temperature, bring a pan of water to the boil and keep it at a steady, rolling boil. You might want to boil the water in a kettle before adding to the pan, which tends to be more energy efficient. Using a slotted spoon or fish slice, gently lower some of the dough rings into the water. As they all need to be at the surface, you won't be able to do them all at once unless your pan is enormous. After about a minute, use the slotted spoon to turn the dough rings over and leave for about another minute. Remove the rings from the water, allow the excess water to drip and steam for a few seconds, place them on a well-greased baking tray and bake for about 10-15 minutes.

Campfire damper

Damper might have originated in Australia, perhaps inspired by breads made from indigenous seeds by First Nations people, and maybe gained its name from a Lancastrian dialect word. Whatever its history, damper has been enjoyed in many countries by generations of backwoods people, youth groups and other outdoor types. Now often made with self-raising flour or the addition of baking powder, damper can be made using baker's yeast, beer, or left unleavened.

Only light a fire with the landowner's permission. Children (and the campfire) should be supervised at all times. Also with the landowner's permission, cut twigs about 50-100cm long and 10mm in diameter from a non-poisonous tree or bush, such as hazel, oak or willow. Use a book or website to help you identify any of these or others you're unsure about. Either strip the bark of the twigs or wipe them clean.

Divide the dough into eight or ten pieces, roll into balls and roll each into a sausage shape between one and two centimetres in diameter. Pinch one end of each piece of dough against one end of each twig, then wind the dough around and along the stick in a spiral, before pinching the other end against the twig to hold it in place. Leave the dough to prove while you set up and light the fire. Once way to do this is sticking the non-dough end of the twig in the ground, placing a carrier bag over the doughy end (trapping air inside so it doesn't touch) and tying the bag around the twig.

Cooking over flames tends to result in food that's sooty and maybe charred on the outside and undercooked inside, so wait until the fire has burnt down to glowing embers. Remove the carrier bag, pick up the stick and hold the doughy end above the embers, twirling it continuously or at least every minute. It needs to be close enough to cook but far enough away that it doesn't burn. It's a good idea to wear non-synthetic gloves to prevent your hands from getting uncomfortably hot. The dough should take between about 15 and 20 minutes to cook through. If you can find a stick with a fork, you can use it to prop up your cooking stick, rather than having to hold it in the air the whole time. Holding the dough with an oven mitt or folded tea towel, slide it off the twig. It's good served with a campfire stew or the Scouts' favourite – jam.

Once you've finished, remember to extinguish the embers fully with water, stirring through with a stick or garden spade/fork to ensure all the ashes are soaked. Make sure you don't leave behind any food scraps or other litter.

Chapati or roti

Use of these words varies, as do recipes for them. Some people will call what follows a chapati, some a roti and others will say it's neither. Omit the yeast and salt from the basic dough recipe. After kneading, cover the dough and leave it to rest for at least 30 minutes. If necessary, it can be left for hours at room temperature, or up to a few days in the fridge. Divide the dough into balls weighing about 30-40g and roll each into a circle – see page 49.

The next part should be done by a responsible adult, not a child. Heat a tawa, frying pan or griddle and slide one of the flour-dusted dough circles onto it. Cook for about 15-30 seconds, flip the dough over using a fish slice or heat-proof spatula and cook for about another 30 seconds. Flip and cook for a few more seconds and repeat until there are brown spots on both sides. The trick is to get the pan hot enough to cook the roti quickly enough that it remains soft and flexible but not so hot that it scorches the dough. Pile the cooked flatbreads on top of each other, wrapped in a teatowel to trap some of the escaping steam, which helps to keep them soft. Some people brush these in butter, oil or ghee while warm.

Pita/pitta

After the first proof, divide the dough into about 10 pieces and roll into balls. Dust the worksurface and each ball with flour and shape each into a circle (see page 49) or oval about 4mm thick using a rolling pin. Cover and leave for about 30 minutes. Place a baking tray or baking/pizza stone in the oven and heat to 230–250°C. Place the flour-dusted dough circles onto the heated tray/stone and bake for a few minutes until they puff up. They won't brown much, if at all. Remove the pitas from the oven and pile them on top of each other, wrapped in a teatowel to trap some of the escaping steam, which helps to keep them soft.

Pizza

Wholemeal pizza bases are not common but are a great way to combine breadmaking with other cooking skills. Depending on the age, ability and skill levels of the child/ren, they can slice, chop and grate toppings and perhaps even help you to make a tomato sauce while the dough is proving. At its simplest, this can be tinned tomatoes blended (or smushed up by hand) into a sauce as smooth or textured as you/they like, or a jar of passata. Toppings also give you a huge range of things to taste and talk about with the child/ren – general food education books, websites, videos etc. will help you way beyond the scope of this book.

After the first proof, place a baking tray or baking/pizza stone in the oven and heat to about 200°–220°C. Divide the dough into equal-sized pieces for two or more bases. Using a rolling pin or just hands, shape each into more or less a circle (or rectangle, oval or any other shape, really) between 3mm and 10mm thick, depending on your preference for a thin or thick base. Slide each base onto a peel (see page 44) dusted with flour, cornmeal or rice flour. Spread each base with tomato sauce, sprinkle or place any other topping being used over the sauce, then sprinkle with grated cheese. Transfer the pizza(s) from the peel onto the baking stone or tray. It's a knack that involves touching the end of the peel onto the far side of the stone, then whipping it back to leave the pizza where you want it – a bit like that trick of whipping away a tablecloth to leave everything standing on the table. Alternatively, pizzas can be shaped and topped on a baking tray that's been oiled or lined with baking paper. Bake for about 10 minutes and check. If it's not done, rotate the pizza(s) by 180 degrees and bake for a few minutes more before checking again.

Slow dough

Using cool water and less yeast means the dough will take longer to prove and be ready to bake. Spreading the stages of the breadmaking process across a day, rather than having to be around to do them all over the course of a few hours, can be useful to fit them around your day. For example, you can make the dough at around eight or nine in the morning; give it a stretch and fold during a mid-morning break and perhaps again at lunchtime; shape it at about two or three in the afternoon and then bake at around five or six in the evening. While the oven is on, you can use it to make your evening meal before or after baking the dough.

Use water straight from the tap and only a third of the yeast shown in the recipe. Alternatively, you can multiply the other ingredients by three. Using this recipe and method for 1.5kg of flour (which happens to be the most common size of bags sold for homebakers) will produce enough dough to make two large loaves and a large pizza. This book's author knows so because it's what he does more or less every Saturday.

Staffordshire oatcakes

This is an odd one out amongst these recipes as it uses equal quantities of flour and oats. It's a good one if you don't have access to an oven, if the flour you have grown turns out not to be strong enough to make a high-rising loaf, or simply because you love oatcakes.

Ingredients

Makes about 5 x 23cm oatcakes

- 100g porridge oats (not instant porridge)
- 100g wholemeal flour
- 2g fresh yeast (or about 1g dried active)
- 350g milk, water or mixture of the two
- 2g salt (a bit less than half a teaspoon)
- A little oil to grease the griddle or pan

Equipment

- Scales
- Large mixing bowl
- Large plastic bag
- Griddle or heavy-bottomed frying pan, ideally about 25-30cm in diameter
- Hob (gas or electric)
- Ladle
- Fish slice
- Wire cooling rack and clean tea towel

Method

1. Put all of the ingredients into a bowl and stir to make a thick batter.
2. Cover the bowl and leave to ferment for about 60 minutes or until bubbles form at the surface of the batter.
3. Oil the griddle or heavy-bottomed frying pan lightly, and place over a medium heat.
4. Ladle in the batter and swirl around to form a pancake about 3mm thick.
5. Cook until the batter sets and bubbles pop through the surface like those in a crumpet or pikelet.
6. Flip over with a spatula or fish slice and cook for about a minute more.

Use them as you'd use a pancake, tortilla, chapatti or other flatbread: flat, rolled or folded with the filling of your choice. They're best hot but can be eaten cold. Oatcakes can be stored in an airtight container in the fridge for a day or two. To freeze, layer them between sheets of greaseproof paper, seal in a bag or container and freeze flat.

Sourdough bread

Rather than being an ingredient or a particular type of bread, sourdough is a process; it's the oldest way of making dough rise.

Despite the name, sourdough bread doesn't have to be sour. If you've tried a loaf with a pronounced tang, that was down to the baker choosing to make it that way or perhaps not knowing how to control the acidity. Every type or style of bread that can be made using fresh or dried baker's yeast can be made using a sourdough starter. Want to use your starter to make brioche? Go for it!

The sourdough process takes time but most of it's not your time. While the dough has to put in the hours, you only have to put in the minutes. You do bits here and there and get on with your life in between.

Dough monster!

How to nurture your very own bubbling, burping, breadmaking buddy.

Genuine sourdough bread is leavened using only a culture of yeasts and 'friendly' lactic acid bacteria. These live all around us, including thriving communities on the surface of cereal grains. When you milled your wheat, these microbes were incorporated into the flour, where they're lying more or less dormant. All you need to do to rouse them from their snoozing is to give them the right conditions – warm and wet.

A plastic container with a press-on lid makes a good lair for your dough monster. If it gets a bit frisky, the lid will simply pop off.

Days one to five (ish)

- 30g flour per day
- 30g water (at about 20°C) per day

The quantity of flour you use isn't all that important but try to keep to the 1:1 ratio. On each of the first five days, add equal amounts of flour and water into your container, mix, close and leave at room temperature (again about 20°C) for 24 hours.

For the first few days, the mixture might seem lifeless and could smell vinegary or even a bit iffy. Don't worry about this as it should soon start bubbling and the smell will develop into something yeasty and maybe even floral.

Day six (ish)

Once your dough monster is burping and bubbling nicely, you can grab a bit of it to make sourdough bread. This usually takes about four to seven days but might take more or less. If it's not bubbling by day six, keep repeating the flour and water addition until it is.

Your dough monster is now ready to help you make sourdough bread. After you use some, simply add back equal amounts of flour and water. Bakers call this feeding or refreshing. You also need to refresh it on the day before a baking session.

Caring for your dough monster

Your dough monster is a living thing (well, technically billions of living things) so get to know it. The acidity, flavour, aromas and speed at which starters work vary, so learn what's normal for yours. You might want to experiment with different ratios and total amounts of flour to water in your refreshments. A wetter starter will ferment more quickly than a stiff one. Refreshing it more often, or adding a lot of flour and water to a small amount of starter, will dilute the flavour and acidity.

Unlike pets, you or other members of your household, your dough monster doesn't necessarily have to be fed frequently. Though it will need refreshing at least once a day if you leave it at room temperature, it can be left to its own devices in the fridge for weeks or even months, because the low temperature slows the microbes' metabolism right down. Don't worry if the flour settles, leaving a layer of brownish liquid on top. This is just gravity working its magic and is normal. You can either stir it back into your starter or pour it off. If your dough monster hasn't been used for a while, the second option is probably better as the liquid (sometimes known as hooch) will have started to become alcoholic, which can inhibit the microbes and make your bread taste a bit odd.

If your dough monster has been napping in the fridge for yonks, you might need to pour some away and start refreshing a few days before a baking session. If it's been months or years (the author once forgot his for about two years) then scoop out just a spoonful from the bottom, put it into a new container and start the refreshments. It should be back up to the job in a few days.

What's your dough monster called?

Not every baker names their sourdough starter but many do. Ones we've seen include Bread Pitt, Bao Tse Tung, Clint Yeastwood, Ayeasta Franklin, Bread Sheeran, Shah Rukh Naan and Olivia Gluten John. Will you think of a name for yours?

Simple sourdough bread

Three ingredients equal a world of bread!

Ingredients

Makes one large (about 800g) loaf, or a couple of small ones.

Leaven

- 100g sourdough starter (equal weights of flour and water)*
- 100g wholemeal flour
- 100g water

*Refreshed/fed and bubbling like a good 'un.

Dough

- 300g leaven (the combination of all of the ingredients above)
- 400g wholemeal flour
- 250g water
- 6g salt (about one level 5ml teaspoon)

Equipment

- Scales
- Mixing bowl
- Plastic bag (or tea towel)
- Loaf tin or baking tray
- Oven
- Oven gloves
- Cooling rack

Method

1. Make the leaven by combining the three ingredients in a bowl, covering and leaving for about 10–12 hours (e.g. overnight) at room temperature, until bubbling.
2. Weigh the water in a bowl and stir in the salt until dissolved, then mix in the leaven and flour. There's no need to knead – you can stop once you have a shaggy-looking dough, with no dry flour left. If using plain (rather than bread/strong) flour, read the tips on pages 46 and 47 about developing gluten.
3. Cover the bowl (e.g. with a carrier bag that you can reuse again and again) and leave to rest for about 30 minutes.

4. Scoop the dough out of the bowl with a wetted dough scraper, or your hand, stretch it and fold it in half, then repeat this action. You can find online videos demonstrating how. Place the dough back in the bowl and cover again.
5. Leave at room temperature to prove/rise. Depending on what temperature your room is (the room was about 20–21°C when this bread was tested) this might be six to eight hours. Watch the dough, not the clock – if it doesn't seem to have risen enough, leave it longer.
6. During this time, repeat the stretch'n'fold action every now and then. You could do it hourly or every other hour but it doesn't have to be that often.
7. Shape the dough however you like, e.g. for an oiled tin, banneton, or free-standing on an oiled baking tray. Again, the Internet is full of how-to videos. Cover and leave for two or three hours until it's fully risen.
8. Heat the oven (with a baking stone or tray in place if you're proving dough in a banneton) to about 220–250°C.
9. Turn out the dough if proved in a banneton, dust the top with flour, if you like, and/or slash it with a lame/grignette or very sharp knife and put straight into the oven.
10. Bake a large loaf for about 45 minutes, or small ones for about 30 minutes, turning the temperature down after 10 minutes to about 220°C if you started higher. Turn out onto a wire rack and leave to cool before slicing – bread can be gummy and lose a lot of moisture if you cut when hot.

No-knead bread

This long-rise, higher hydration recipe is ideal for people who have difficulty kneading, and almost everyone can enjoy the full-flavoured, chewy loaf, with a glossy crust that it produces. See the no-knead notes on page 46.

Ingredients

Makes one large loaf.

- 500g wholemeal flour
- 400g warm water (at about 20°C, but this doesn't have to be precise)
- 50g sourdough starter
- 5g salt (about a level teaspoon, or slightly less)
- A little oil and extra flour

Equipment

- Scales
- Mixing bowl
- Plastic bag (or tea towel)

- Casserole dish, Dutch pot or other thick-walled cooking vessel with a lid
- Baking paper/parchment
- Oven
- Oven gloves
- Cooling rack

Method

1. Dissolve the salt in the water and stir all ingredients together until they form a sloppy dough.
2. Cover the bowl with a bag or damp tea towel (allowing space for the dough to rise and not touch) and leave the dough to prove. The dough is ready once it has puffed up in the bowl and bubbles appear on the surface, though it won't quite have doubled in size, as is usually called for in bread recipes. The time it takes will vary, mainly due to room temperature and how frisky the starter is feeling. It might be about:

   - 14 hours / overnight in the fridge (made using cold water)
   - 6 hours at room temperature in the summer (21–24°C)
   - 10 hours at room temperature in the winter (18°C)

3. Oil a sheet of baking parchment well and dust with plenty of flour. Push it, oil side up, into a bowl that's a little smaller than your cooking pot, trying to minimise the creases.
4. Get your hands wet to stop the dough sticking to them and scrape around the inside of the bowl to release the dough. Grab the dough from underneath at east and west, stretch out slightly until you have flaps long enough to push into the centre. Repeat from north and south. Lift out the dough and dump, flaps down, into the paper-lined bowl.
5. Cover and leave to prove again for about an hour. About 30 minutes into this second proof, place the cooking pot (and lid) into the oven and crank it up as high as it will go to build up plenty of heat.
6. Slide the pot out of the oven and quickly but carefully remove the lid, grab the baking parchment by four corners and dump (paper side down) it and the dough into the pot, replace the lid and slide the pot back into the oven.
7. After 20 minutes, remove the lid, turn the oven down to about 220°C and bake for another 20–25 minutes. This bread has a fairly high water content, so it's safe to err on the side of a bit longer, rather than end up with a loaf that's under-baked in the middle.
8. Remove the loaf from the pot, peel off the baking parchment and leave the bread to cool on a wire rack.

Breadcrumb bread

As this recipe uses half the usual amount of flour, and a tiny amount of yeast, it's handy if you're running low on either. It uses the sponge and dough method, which once was very common in small, local bakeries around the UK. You could instead use the basic Real Bread recipe at the start of this section, replacing up to half of the flour with breadcrumbs.

Ingredients

Makes one medium (about 650g) loaf.

- The sponge
- 60g strong/bread, or plain, flour (white, brown or wholemeal)
- 60g water
- 3g fresh (or 1g / ¼tsp fast acting) yeast*

*Read the label and avoid brands that contain any additives.

The dough

- 200g stale/leftover bread
- 200g strong/bread, or plain, flour (white, brown or wholemeal)
- 220-250g water straight from the tap
- 120g sponge (i.e. the combination of all of the sponge ingredients above)
- 6g salt (about one level 5ml teaspoon)

Equipment

- Scales
- Mixing bowl
- Plastic bag (or tea towel)
- Bread tin OR proving basket plus a baking tray or stone
- Lame/grignette or very sharp knife
- Oven
- Oven gloves
- Cooling rack

Method

1. Make the sponge by combining the three ingredients in a bowl, covering and leaving for about 10-12 hours (e.g. overnight) at room temperature, until bubbling. Alternatively, leave out the sponge stage and make a straight dough with about 5g of fresh (or 2-3g / 1tsp instant) yeast instead - see below.

2. Cut or tear the stale bread into chunks, then blitz into crumbs using a blender or food processor.
3. Weigh the water in a bowl and stir in the salt until dissolved, then mix in the sponge, breadcrumbs, flour and (if you've gone for the straight dough version) yeast. There's no need to knead – you can stop once you have a shaggy-looking dough but there's no dry flour left.
4. Cover the bowl (e.g. with a large plastic bag that you can reuse again and again) and leave to rest for 30 minutes or so.
5. Scoop the dough out of the bowl with a wetted dough scraper, or your hand, stretch it and fold it in half, then repeat this action. Place the dough back in the bowl and cover again.
6. Leave at room temperature to prove/rise. Depending on what temperature your room is this might be six to eight hours. During this time, repeat the stretch and fold action every now and then. You could do it hourly or every other hour but it doesn't have to be that often.
7. Shape the dough however you like, e.g. for an oiled tin, banneton, or free-standing on an oiled baking tray. Cover and leave for two or three hours until it's fully risen.
8. Heat the oven (with a baking stone or tray in place if you're proving dough in a banneton) to about 250°C.
9. Turn out the dough if proved in a banneton, dust the top with flour, if you like, and/or slash it with a lame/grignette or very sharp knife and put straight into the oven.
10. Bake a large loaf for about 45–60 minutes, turning the heat down to about 220°C after the first 15 minutes. Turn out onto a wire rack and leave to cool before slicing.

Storing bread

Always let bread cool completely before putting it away. Hot or even slightly warm bread will give off steam, which will condense on the inside of a container or wrapper. This dampness might make the bread soggy and can encourage the growth of mould.

Although the low temperature in a fridge might slow down the growth of mould, it will accelerate staling. Also, if there is too much of a difference between the temperatures of the loaf and the fridge, it can also cause condensation to form inside the loaf bag.

Bread bin

A good place to store bread that you are going to eat in a day or two is a bread bin. A loose-fitting lid will mean the bread doesn't dry out, whilst allowing any excess moisture to escape.

Freezing

Bread keeps very well if put in a plastic bag or container and kept in the freezer. Slice it first so you can defrost and use it a piece at a time. Putting frozen bread somewhere too warm (e.g. in the oven) or in a microwave to defrost can cause it to dry out. It's better to leave at room temperature to thaw slowly.

Leftovers

In the unlikely event that you manage not to scoff all of your yummy Real Bread before it goes stale, don't throw it away!

You can revive a stale, large loaf by putting it in a hot oven (200-220°C) for around five minutes, or a small one at around 170°C for about twelve to fifteen minutes. Turning an oven on just to do this seems a waste, though, and the bread needs to be used straight away as it will get even more stale very quickly after this treatment.

Instead, ways to recycle stale bread are almost endless. They include:

- toast.
- bruschetta.
- croutons.
- eggy bread (also known as French toast).
- bread pudding.
- brown bread ice cream.

...or made into Real Breadcrumbs, which can be used to make bread sauce, and stuffings or crumb coatings for all sorts of things. Fresh breadcrumbs can be frozen, or you can spread them onto a baking tray, dry them out in the oven (with the door open) once you've turned it off after baking, then store in an airtight container.

Using leftovers doesn't solve the enormous global problem of food waste but it's a start. It's also a great way into conversations with children about the issue. You can find some stale bread recipes on our website and in our book **Slow Dough: Real Bread**.

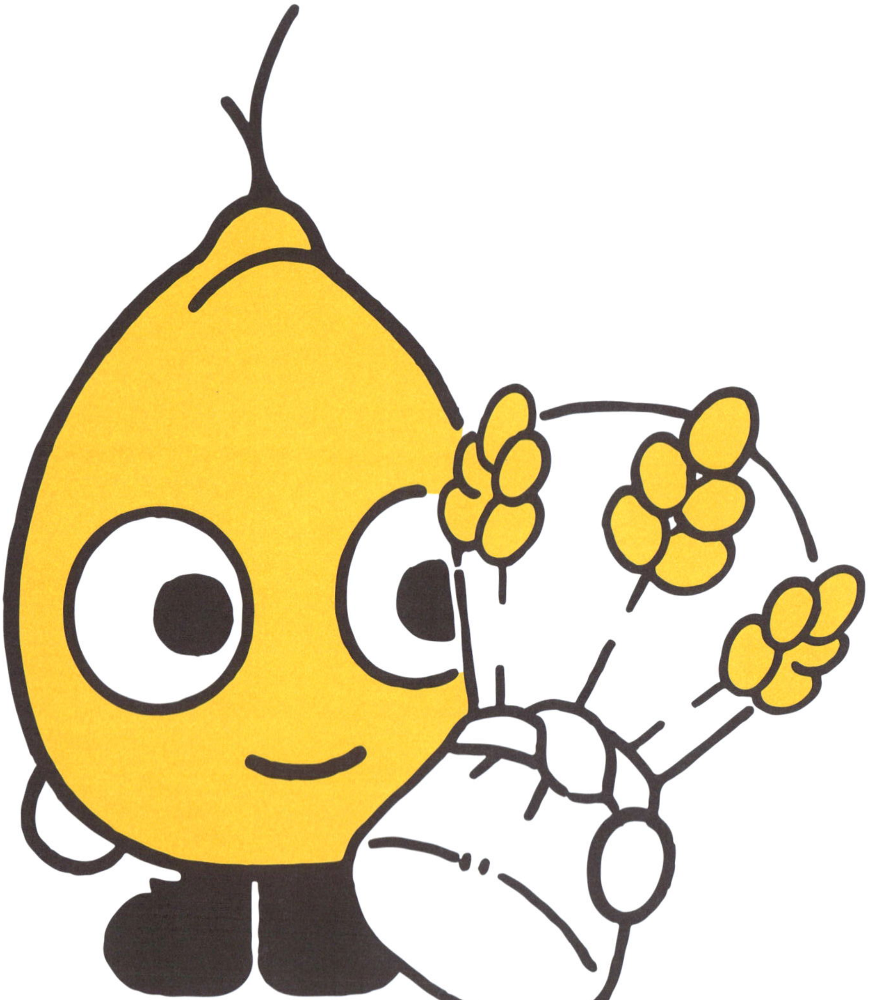

Field notes

The following articles are by people involved in running seed to sandwich projects with children. Longer versions of these originally appeared in the Real Bread Campaign supporters' magazine True Loaf.

Bakers' Bush

During her time as deputy head of Greenside Primary in Shepherd's Bush, west London, Georgina Webber was the driving force behind a pioneering whole-school approach to food.

Our journey towards breaducation and setting up our own microbakery at Greenside Primary School has been an eight year one. In 2015, we decided that we were not happy with the standard of the school lunches served by the local authority catering contractor, so decided to bring catering in-house.

This same philosophy extends out to the school garden, where we have a vegetable growing area. When we took control of the kitchen, we began growing some vegetables but wanted to make more of this amazing resource. We turned the garden into a science project that the whole school is involved in and began embedding it in our curriculum.

We thought about what we could do next, which is when the idea of a microbakery came in. We wanted to involve our whole school community in a project that would unite us through collective action. It would be one to help develop our knowledge and understanding of both food production and the food system. We wanted to show that good bread is for everyone.

Getting kitted out

We rallied our school community to clear some ground at the front of the school, right on the street, where we planted our field of wheat. I say field, but it really is only a patch of about four square metres! With the wheat in the ground, the next thing we needed was some basic kit and, most importantly, a bread oven. Through the support of our Parent Staff Association and generous donations from some of our suppliers, we were able to buy a Rackmaster RM2020 oven, some baskets, dough scrapers and plastic tubs. Our school kitchen already had a Hobart mixer but it didn't (and still doesn't) have a dough hook. We went with what we had and made the plan from there.

We harvested our wheat and whilst we will never be able to make enough flour for all of our bread, we are making an important connection with where our food comes from. The children recognise how good our bread is. We linked breadmaking to whatever learning experience we could: learning about climatic conditions needed for growing wheat in geography lessons; making Ancient Egyptian bread in history, making sourdough pizza to inspire a travel guide to San Francisco; the list goes on! I showed all the teachers how to make bread so that they could bake with their own pupils.

We wanted ours to become a community oven and have invited pupils' families to come and bake their bread with us. Everyone is welcome and this has proved a great way of bringing people together through bread. Beyond the school day, we bake extra each Friday to share with our community at our weekly bread sales. Rather than charging a set amount, we just ask people to donate what they can afford. The money all goes back into the bakery project. Each week the line snakes around the playground – this is a real validation of what we are doing. As one parent said: "We only buy this bread now, the other stuff just doesn't taste as good."

Playing fields of wheat

School gardening club leader, Liz Read, tells the story of how children grew wheat on their playing field at Holy Trinity Primary Academy in Wiltshire.

The project was sparked in October 2017, when local farmer Emily Pepler gave a talk at a school assembly. She said that our large playing field could produce enough wheat for approximately 15,000 loaves of bread, about one from each square metre. The children thought this was an amazing idea and were disappointed that Mercedes Henning, the headteacher, was not going to give permission to plough the whole thing up! Given the pupils' disappointment, she and I devised a whole school project around growing a smaller plot of wheat.

The maintenance contractors rotovated two spaces in the playing field, each about three metres by two metres. A grass path was left in the middle to allow us access to care for the wheat. The path was the same width as the gang mower used to maintain the playing field, ensuring it could be trimmed easily.

In March 2018, we took the children out a class at a time, each child sowing a small number of seeds by hand. Skyfall is a winter, rather than spring, variety and we had accepted that our seeds might not produce much of a crop when sown this late. In fact, we weren't even sure if the seeds would grow at all.

Happily, the wheat grew steadily on the playing field with only a little weeding needed. We gave it no attention over the summer holidays but it was still standing when school returned in September. The children harvested the ripe wheat with their classroom scissors, gathering the very dry and crackly ears in the baskets. The wheat stalks were just mowed by the maintenance team and grass regrew over the plots, leaving no trace of the project.

Harvest festival

At the next assembly, I gave a short talk on the processes so far – ploughing the earth, planting the wheat and harvesting it. The whole school then threshed the ears of wheat by covering them with a tarpaulin and walking up and down over it. This was really effective and a lot of fun. The children winnowed the wheat in the playground using tea towels and sieves to remove the chaff, before grinding the wheat with a small hand-cranked mill. They then made their own Real Bread, each having a chance to knead the communal batch of dough, which was made into a wheatsheaf loaf for the school harvest festival.

Cross-curricular activity

The school used the project as a topic for lessons and activities across the curriculum. The Wiltshire Museum introduced a historical perspective by bringing in agricultural implements. These included two types of stone quern, which the children were able to examine and try using to mill wheat. They also saw a huge scythe, measuring jugs and sieves. This helped the children look at the changing technology used to grow and harvest wheat, appreciate the hard work it took to grind grain by hand. As it is a rural school and some children are in farming families, it helped create a sense of connection with previous generations.

The crochet club made long, woollen chains, to which CDs were attached to ward off birds. The children studied the art of David Hockney, whose work included paintings of wheat fields, and some classes created their own paintings based on this. Religion was explored through the story of Ruth the gleaner.

Enthusiasm and excitement

It was a truly wonderful project and was covered in the local paper, parish newsletter and through talks to local gardening clubs. It had come from the spontaneous enthusiasm of the children, who were included at every stage, and created excitement within the school and elsewhere. We are so glad we took the chance to grow the wheat and will always look back with huge fondness on baking our lawn.

Seed to sandwich in Shaky Toon

Tyra Dempster reports on a Scottish village bakery and primary school collaboration she helps run as a volunteer.

Each morning, a handful of children at Comrie Primary School spend half an hour making Real Bread. They rotate every day, giving each of the rural Scottish village school's 130 or so pupils the opportunity to make, bake, slice and enjoy loaves they've nurtured from being seeds in the ground.

Named after being inspired by the work at Greenside Primary in London, Breaducation at Comrie Primary School is the result of a three-year collaboration with Wild Hearth, our local artisan bakery. In 2020, the bakery's founder John Castley began inviting small groups of pupils from the school to sow and grow a small plot of wheat. They returned in the autumn to harvest, thresh and mill their crop, finally visiting the bakery to make Real Bread from the flour. John also invited to the school a straw weaving specialist, who taught every pupil how to make a hairst (harvest) knot, traditionally given as a token of love or luck.

The following year, more pupils became involved to help to sow grain over a much larger area; as the wheat grew, so did the project. We began to wonder if we could turn this soil-to-slice initiative into a daily part of school life. We hoped that the children having this practical experience would help them to understand more about the health and nutritional qualities of the food they eat.

Pupil power

The headteacher, Heather White, enthusiastically welcomed the project. She supported a bakery-led pupil consultation and blind taste tests to create a bread that the children could make according to their tastes and preferences. The pupils threw themselves into the development discussion, whilst demolishing every crumb of bread in the taste tests, and we emerged with a clear brief. The children voted overwhelmingly to make bread from locally grown grain as they believed this was more environmentally sustainable. Their taste test result was firmly for a loaf with a complex flavour profile that was based on a rustic, French wholemeal bread. We were delighted with our brief and couldn't have hoped for a better combination! Now we had to design a bread that met the pupils' criteria whilst being simple enough for them to make during the school day. Many, many test bakes followed.

We finally arrived at a loaf that fitted the bill, in which half of the flour is from wheat grown by the children and half is from Mungoswells in nearby East Lothian.

It is leavened by a sourdough starter made from Scotland the Bread rye flour, which the children nurture, with a little bit of baker's yeast. The mixing and proving process is simple and it slots into the school schedule. Each day a handful of the children take their turn to make, bake, and slice the bread, which they have named The Shaky Toon Loaf because Comrie is known locally for its occasional wee earthquakes. They then deliver it around the school and have the fun of watching their fellow pupils eating it at break and lunchtime.

Loaf lessons for life

Breaducation at Comrie Primary School offers every pupil a healthy bite at lunch and snack time and teaches them so much more than just how to grow grain and make bread. They also gain a better understanding of ingredients and learn about the nutritional and health benefits of making food from scratch. Weighing and measuring gives them a chance to put maths to practical use, while maintaining a sourdough culture and proving dough offers them an introduction to the biology of microbial cultures and fermentation. It also offers up an introduction to professional skills. The experience of baking may lead to some children to consider it as a career. Some might love the experience of running a bread stall at the school gates and others might enjoy the marketing angle. At the very least, we hope that every Comrie Primary School pupil will hold onto the valuable life skill of making a simple loaf of bread from scratch.

As the project continues, support for it grows. This year we received an offer from a local farmer to grow more wheat for us and we hope to develop many more opportunities for breadmaking with the children. We're in the process of setting up a charity, Breaducation Scotland, and have secured a grant to buy a bread oven for the school. This will allow us to make loaves and additional treats that pupils will be able to sell them on a pay-what-you-can-afford basis at the school gate every Friday to raise money to cover the ingredient and electricity costs. Pupils now run an Instagram account to keep people in our community updated on the project's development and when bread is available to buy.

In February 2023, we nervously submitted our Shaky Toon Loaf to the Scottish Bread Championship and were thrilled when it won a silver medal! We're now working to help the project's roots to become established so that Breaducation settles in as a firm part of primary school life.

From seed to sourdough

The Hackney School of Food's Tom Walker on growing, milling and baking a microplot of wheat with school children.

In September 2021, we invited the Wildfarmed team to join children from Mandeville Primary School for a day of planting and baking. We rolled up our sleeves and weighed out the flour, salt, water and yeast to start making lunch for everyone. As the dough proved in the kitchen, we harvested the toppings from our growing beds. With the heat roaring in our outdoor wood oven, we fired the freshly prepared pizzas, fuelling ourselves up for an afternoon of farming.

Having cleared the weeds from a fifteen-metre-square patch and prepared guide strings for planting straight rows, our Head Gardener, Lidka D'Agostino guided us on drilling holes with bamboo dibbers. We then dropped a mixture of wheat, barley, rye and oat seeds into the holes. We scattered cover crop seeds amongst the rows to out-compete weeds and lock nutrients into the soil. The children enjoyed the hard-work, with one 8-year-old commenting: "I feel like a real farmer today, it's interesting to see how flour is grown."

Early harvest

After our labours, we stood back and watched the slow process of growth throughout the seasons; from first shoots peeking through in the autumn, to brushing snow off the crop during winter. As the year turned warmer, the stalks began their headlong rush to the sky and we charted the growth with different ages of schoolchildren standing amid the stalks. Eventually even the tallest pupil was obscured as some stalks reached two metres high! As mid-summer 2022 approached, we waited for the right moment to harvest, mesmerised by the crop waving in the wind as the heavy ears of the seed heads drooped and turned golden.

As the school year neared its end in June, we invited more children to harvest our microplot. They scythed the wheat, cutting stalks at their base to create straw that we'd use as bedding in our chicken coop, saving the ears, or 'plaits' as Lidka told us they're known as in Poland. Our wonderful volunteer Rima taught us to bundle up the sheafs to be hung and dried over the summer holiday. We even used barley stalks as drinking straws to quench our thirst.

Back to the grindstone

Returning in late summer, we entered the final stages of our journey. The ears were put into paper bags and given a hard shake to release the seeds, an energetic job done with great enthusiasm by the children. After sifting the seed to remove chaff and dust, we headed into our kitchen to discover ancient methods of milling. Our rotary quern was a particular favourite as a simple, effective method with lots of eager hands to turn the millstone, and tangible excitement as the fresh flour poured out. We experimented by smashing some of the larger grains using mortar and pestle to create an even finer wholemeal flour.

Once the flour was ready, we got to the real staff of life - making bread. This time using a sourdough starter for our baking, we weighed, stirred and kneaded with gusto to develop an airy-soft dough. When it came to shaping, imaginations ran free and we saw creations such as plaited mermaid tails, a family of spikey hedgehog rolls, and even pesto and mozzarella stuffed picnic crowns. As one baker said: "I didn't realise you could make so many shapes with dough, I thought plaits were just for hair!"

Following the life cycle from seed-to-sourdough was an eye opening and enthralling experience for everyone at each step. That an inner-city plot of land, a stone's throw away from primary school classrooms, could be used to show hands-on farming was an incredible sight.

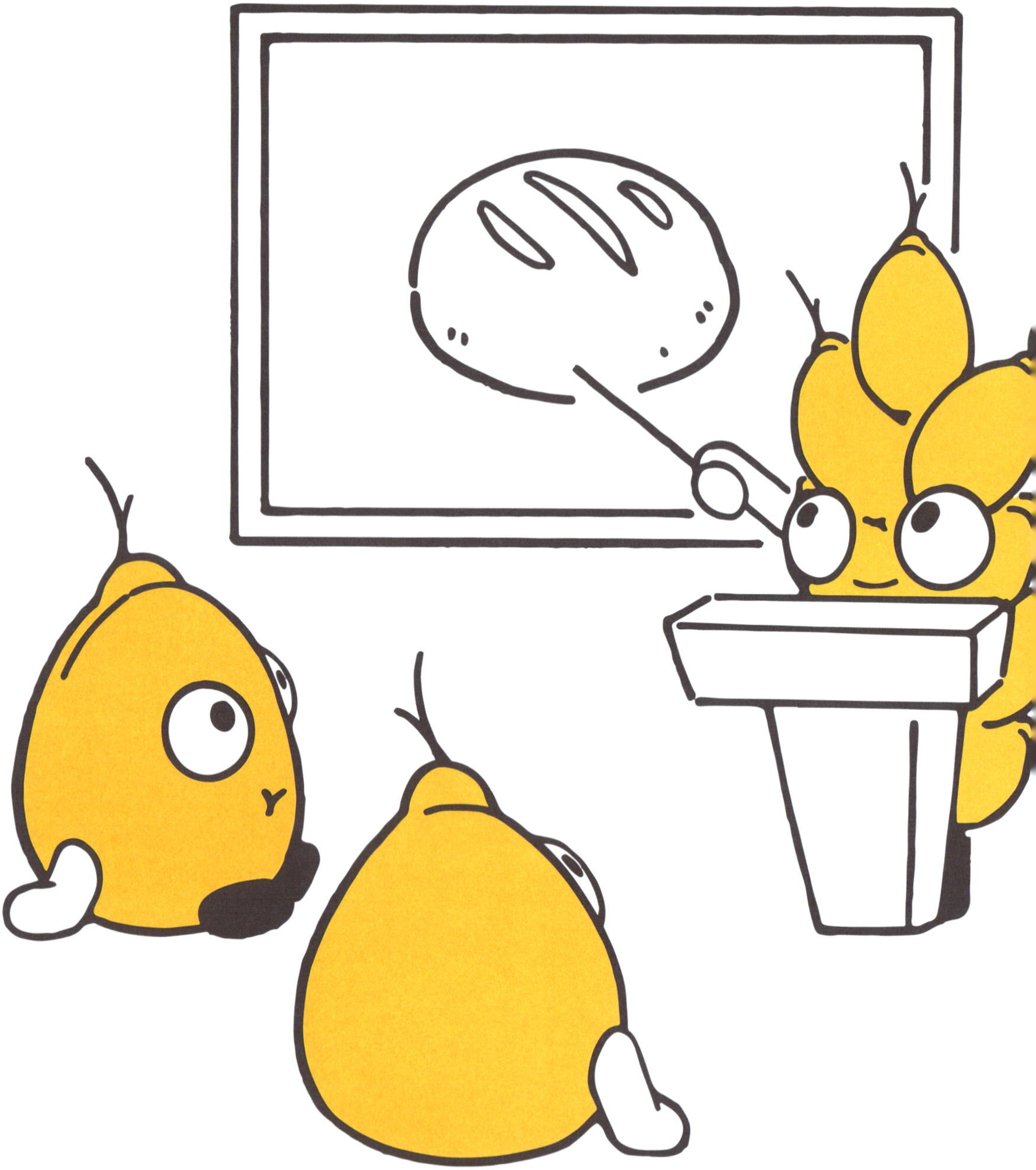

Lessons in Loaf

This section of the book draws upon Lessons in Loaf, the first project and guide created by the Real Bread Campaign in 2010. It was aimed mainly at teachers of primary school children aged around seven to eleven at Key Stage 2 of the National Curriculum in England. For the book, we've broadened the focus and some of the notes might be suitable for use with older children: at Key Stage 3, feeding into GCSE food preparation and nutrition, for example.

As with the rest if this book, you might want or need to adapt some parts according to age, ability, context and facilities available. You might also decide some elements are simply for your own information and interest.

Indoor wheat growing

This project is adapted from teachers' notes produced by the Brockwell Bake Association.

Curriculum subject

Science.

Learning objective

To observe the development of the wheat plant, both above and below ground in order to understand how plants take up moisture and nutrients.

Equipment

For each child or group:

- A straight-sided, 2-litre, transparent plastic bottle
- A plate or tray/container to stand the bottle on/in
- A few handfuls of soil
- A large handful of coarse gravel
- About 10 grains of seed wheat

This experiment is best done with a modern wheat variety, as when fully grown there will be less chance of the bottle and wheat toppling over.

Preparing the bottle

- Remove the label, cut the top off just below where it begins to taper, make five or six drainage holes in the bottom. Depending on the age and ability of the child(ren), you might want to do this step yourself.
- Add gravel to a depth of about 5cm.
- Fill the bottle with soil, to about 5cm from the top.

Sowing

- Evenly space around 10 wheat seeds on top of the soil.
- Cover the wheat with about 2cm of soil.
- Place the bottle on the plate/tray in a sunny position, where it won't get disturbed.
- Add about a mugful of water to the bottle.
- Water again once or twice a week as needed to keep the soil moist but not wet.

Wheat diaries

Help the child(ren) to record the progress of the wheat plants every day for the first week or two. After that you might prefer to switch to weekly observations.

When sown outdoors in Britain, wheat can take six months or more to reach maturity. Growing inside will speed this process a little but will still take months – it's not like growing cress!

- Draw and write notes on the appearance of the plants.
- Measure the plants and calculate their average height, then plot this on a graph.
- You could also calculate the amount the plants have grown since the previous measurement and plot this on the graph as well.

If you have a number of bottles, you could do the following at three-weekly intervals:

- Carefully remove the wheat plants from one bottle. You might need to cut the bottle open.
- Gently clean the soil away from the roots.
- Weigh each of the plants, calculate the average and plot on a graph.
- Measure the length of the roots, calculate the average and plot on a graph.
- Draw the root structure.

After about a month you could change the growing conditions of wheat in one or more of the bottles, for example by:

- Stopping watering.
- Moving to a dark cupboard.
- Moving outside.
- Moving to a fridge.

The child(ren) then record their observations and compare them to the control plants – those in an indoor, sunny position being watered regularly.

Questions

Things you might ask the children to think about could include:

- What do the roots do?
- What do the leaves do?
- Where do these (and other) plants get their water, nutrients and energy?
- What makes the leaves green?

How does your garden grow?

If you have access to enough space and wheat seeds, you might want to divide your plot into a number of equally sized sections (or set up identical pots/planters) for an experiment.

Curriculum subject

Science.

Learning objective

To compare any differences in growth and yields between plots of wheat grown under different conditions.

Equipment

Growing plot, wheat seeds and gardening equipment – see the 'Grow' chapter, starting on page 11.

One plot/section will be your control. For each of the other sections, you vary just one factor, such as:

- Wheat variety.
- Whether or not you use compost.

- How much water you apply.
- Growing in partial shade or full sun.
- Soil type – if you can obtain more than one.

Wheat diaries

Record the growth of the wheat in each plot/section, measuring and charting its height each month. At harvest time, you can weigh and compare the final yield of grain from each section after threshing and winnowing. You might want to go into more detail by selecting 10 or 20 ears from each section, weighing each ear, counting the number of grains on each ear, then calculating and comparing the average figures for each plot.

Ask the child(ren) to consider the reasons for any differences they have recorded.

Yeast balloons

This can be demonstrated by an adult or carried out by the child(ren).

Curriculum subject

Science, food preparation and nutrition.

Learning objective

To see that yeast produces a gas and find out what that gas is.

Equipment and ingredients

- 10g dried active yeast (or 1 sachet fast-acting or 15g fresh)
- 200g warm water
- 15g caster sugar (dissolves more easily than table sugar)
- Balloon
- Small funnel
- Stopwatch, clock or other timer
- Plastic bottle (300ml to 1 litre in capacity)

Method

- For a better chance of the balloon inflating, relax it by blowing it up and letting it deflate two or three times.
- Using the funnel, add the yeast, sugar and water to the bottle. Add the water last or the other things will stick.

- Screw the lid onto the bottle tightly and shake to mix everything together.
- Remove the lid and attach the balloon to the mouth of the bottle, getting it right over the lip all the way around.
- Start the stopwatch.
- Make a note of the appearance of the liquid in the bottle and the balloon. Repeat this every ten minutes for an hour.

Discussion

Q: What did you see?

A: Hopefully, bubbles began to appear in the liquid and the balloon got bigger.

Q: Why did this happen?

A: The yeast cells fed on the sugar, producing carbon dioxide as a waste product. The balloon acted like the gluten in wheat bread dough, trapping the gas and swelling up.

For older children, you could carry out this experiment with three bottles: one as above; the second placed near a radiator; and the third with cold water, placed in a fridge or somewhere considerably cooler than room temperature. Ask the children to compare the results and if they know the reason, which is that yeast's metabolic processes (converting sugar to energy, growing, multiplying and producing carbon dioxide as a waste product) happen faster in warmer conditions.

Gluten washing

Curriculum subject

Science, food preparation and nutrition.

Learning objective

To see that gluten is insoluble and can be isolated from dough by washing to remove the starch.

Ingredients and equipment

- 150g white wheat flour
- 90g water
- Small mixing bowl
- Scales

Method

- Mix the flour and water together to make dough.
- Knead the dough until smooth and elastic.
- Wash the starch out of the dough by squeezing and stretching repeatedly, which will make the water appear milky. Change the water periodically and continue washing until the water stays clear.
- Remove the remaining substance (which is mainly gluten) from the bowl and squeeze it to get rid of as much water as possible. Leave the gluten for about 10 minutes to let it relax and release more water.

Discussion

Q: What changes did you see?

A: The water turned milky white.

Q: What do you think caused this?

A: Starch from the dough dispersing in the water.

Q: What do you think is left?

A: Gluten, which is formed when proteins in wheat mix with water.

Q: Why didn't the gluten wash away?

A: Though water is needed to allow the proteins in wheat flour to combine, the gluten that is formed is insoluble.

Q: Is this a reversible or irreversible change?

A: It's an irreversible change.

Follow-on activity

If you are doing this experiment at the same time as baking / cooking in the oven, put the gluten ball on a greased baking tray and bake at about 200°C for around 5-10 minutes until it is puffed up and golden brown. Remove from the oven and allow to cool, then tear or slice it open.

Farming methods

There are many forms and systems of agriculture, each with its pros and cons, as well as principles and practices that overlap those of other types. These are brief notes on some of the practices most commonly used in the UK.

Crop rotation

Traditional methods of farming typically involve a three- or four-year rotation of crops. After wheat, a field might be sown with beans or another nitrogen fixing crop, followed by potatoes the next year. The field may then be left fallow as pasture grazed by animals, or grass left to grow and then cut for hay. Both would allow clover, another nitrogen fixing plant, to grow. The following year might be brassicas (e.g. cabbage, Brussels sprouts, broccoli or cauliflower) or root vegetables, with the cycle then turning back to wheat. The nutrients that plants take out of, and put back into, the soil change each year. It also means that pests and diseases specific to a particular plant don't get their favourite feast year after year, which helps to break the cycle. Rather than rotating crops on a cycle like this, some 'conventional' farmers swap back and forth between two crops, or simply grow the same type year after year. They may use more biocides and artificial fertiliser in attempts to compensate for the lost benefits of rotation.

Agroecological farming

The Soil Association says: 'Ecology is the study of relationships between plants, animals, people, and their environment – and the balance between these relationships. Agroecology is the application of ecological concepts and principals in farming.' Forms of agroecology include organic and biodynamic farming, agroforestry and permaculture.

Organic farming

According to the Soil Association, 'organic farmers work to a strict set of standards, which must legally comply with strict EU regulation, to ensure that their farms sustain the health of: soils, ecosystems, animals and people. These standards are built on the key principles of organic agriculture: health, ecology, care, fairness.' In order to be legally able to use the word organic, producers must follow certain rules and be licensed by an official certification body. Rules for cereal farmers in the UK include bans on weedkillers, artificial fertilisers and genetically modified organisms, as well as restrictions on the type and use of insecticides and fungicides. In some cases, the yield (how much a crop, animals and pieces of land produce) of organic farming might be lower, which can have an effect on pricing – but see the note on hidden costs in the 'conventional' farming section below.

Biodynamic farming

This follows similar principles and rules to organic farming but, according to the Biodynamic Association, 'has metaphysical and spiritual roots that organics does not.' The organisation goes on to say: 'In biodynamic agriculture the farm (or holding) is considered to have its own identity and be a self-sustaining organism in its own right. A fundamental principle which a biodynamic farm works towards is thus to be a "closed loop" system that does not need to buy in feed or fertility from external suppliers, or one that is stretched beyond its natural capacity.' As part of this: 'The use of home made compost (and manures) enlivened with biodynamic herbal preparations is obligatory.' Also 'a biodynamic astronomical calendar can be consulted to help assess optimum times for sowing, planting etc.'

Regenerative agriculture

In general, regenerative farmers focus on improving soil health, working to increase their land's biodiversity and ability to capture and store carbon, though the methods by which they do this varies. Some plough their fields, others minimise or avoid doing so, for example. Unlike organic farming, there is no legal definition (or even general consensus) of exactly what regenerative agriculture is. Some 'regen' farmers will follow principles and practices equivalent to (and maybe beyond) organic or perhaps biodynamic standards. Without regulation, however, the term is more open to being used in 'greenwashing' – marketing that states or implies that environmental standards/practises are better than they are.

Minimum tillage and direct drilling

An increasing number of farmers are turning to minimum or no-tillage systems, meaning they do little to no ploughing between crops, instead drilling seeds of the next crop directly into the soil. While tilling can help improve drainage, frequent major disturbance of the soil has a number of disadvantages. These include destroying soil structure, making it more likely to dry out and prone to erosion; reduction in organic matter, degrading the soil's microbiome; and disturbing beneficial inhabitants such as mycorrhizal fungi and worms.

Reduced tillage reduces use of agricultural machinery, so cuts labour and fuel costs, while a number of studies have concluded it might also reduce greenhouse gas emissions. Some farmers report they have found weeds to be more problematic in no-till cropping, and struggle to control them effectively without the use of chemical herbicides.

Modern industrial farming

This is commonly known as 'conventional' agriculture, which the Oxford Dictionary defines as: 'farming practices that involve the use of chemical fertilisers, pesticides, and machinery.' Key aims include maximising yield/output, which has helped to eradicate famine in the UK and many other countries.

There can be hidden/displaced costs of producing larger quantities of food at lower prices, though. As the US-based Rodale Institute puts it: 'conventional agriculture causes increased greenhouse gas emissions, soil erosion, water pollution, and threatens human health.' By contrast 'organic farming has a smaller carbon footprint, conserves and builds soil health, replenishes natural ecosystems for cleaner water and air, all without toxic pesticide residues.'

What is Real Bread?

This can be done as a whole class activity which can be recorded on the interactive white board/flipchart or done as a paired/group activity.

Curriculum subject

Science, food preparation and nutrition.

Learning objectives

To understand what the essential ingredients of Real Bread are and what they do.

Q: What are the essential ingredients of bread?

A: Flour and water, though salt is usually added and yeast (in one form or another) is often used.

Q: What do these ingredients do in bread?

Flour: Most flour used in the UK is made from wheat. White flour comes from the middle part of the wheat grain and is mostly carbohydrate (mainly starch) and protein (mainly gluten). If we looked under a powerful microscope, we'd see that gluten is made up of coiled up strands that look like mini springs. When water and energy (in the form of kneading) are added, the gluten strands begin to uncoil and start to form links to other strands close by, joining together to form what looks like a net.

As this microscopic mesh develops, forming more and more links, it becomes like bubble gum, able to trap gas. This stretchy network of gluten strands is the main building material of the walls of the holes we see in bread.

The starch in flour provides food for the yeast, as well as acting as more 'building blocks' for the bread. The darker, outer parts of the grain – the brown bits – in wholemeal and brown flour add to the flavour and nutritional quality of bread.

Water is the second main ingredient of bread after flour. It is essential to the process of wheat proteins combining to form gluten and hydrating starch, another key building block of dough. Water also enables other ingredients to dissolve or disperse through the dough and produces steam that helps it to rise.

Yeasts are microscopic, single-celled fungi. There are thought to be at least 1,500, and maybe more than 2,000, species of yeast. Yeast cells occur naturally all around (and inside) us, in the air, in the soil and on other living things, such as cereal grains.

Unleavened bread is made without yeast, while the dough for leavened bread can be made to rise by the yeast in a sourdough starter culture, or by commercially cultivated (usually known as baker's) yeast. A sourdough culture might contain just one or many species of yeast. Baker's yeast is a species called *Saccharomyces cerevisiae*, which means beer sugar fungus as it is the same species used in brewing. It is estimated that one gram of fresh baker's yeast might contain 6-10 billion yeast cells, while one gram of dried active yeast might contain 12-20 billion.

Like humans, yeast cells use carbohydrates for energy to live. In breadmaking, this comes from the starch in the flour. Enzymes in the flour and produced by the yeast turn some of the starch into simpler sugars, which the yeast cells use for energy. This is called fermentation. As a waste product of this process, yeast cells give off carbon dioxide, a bit like we do when we breathe out. In breadmaking, this is the gas that fills the bubbles made by the gluten and starch. Alcohol is also produced, though in breadmaking the amount is very small and it evaporates during and after baking.

Salt is not technically necessary in breadmaking but a little bit helps to boost the flavour. It also has an effect on browning and gluten strength.

Other natural ingredients (such as oils/fats, nuts, seeds, herbs, sugar and eggs) aren't necessary but can be used in Real Bread making to help create particular flavours and textures.

How are different products made?

Most of what is sold as 'bread' in the UK is very, very different from the Real Bread the children have grown.

Curriculum subjects

Science, food preparation and nutrition, citizenship, healthy eating, plus geography and history.

Learning objectives

- Thinking about differences between different methods of manufacture.
- Asking questions about the food they eat.

Materials

A wrapped, sliced, white factory loaf. The longer the list of ingredients and additives, the better – but only for the purpose of this lesson!

Q: How did we make Real Bread?

A: We:

- mixed together flour, water, yeast [or sourdough starter] and a little salt to make dough.
- kneaded the dough by stretching and folding it over and over again.
- left the dough to prove. During this time, the yeast fermented and made the dough rise.
- kneaded the dough again, shaped it and left it to prove again.
- cooked the dough [baked, steamed, griddled, fried, roasted over fire, or however you made it]

Activity

Now let's look at a wrapped, sliced loaf. This was made in a very large factory where all of the baking is done by machines that are controlled by computers. The loaves are made very, very quickly and although each factory makes thousands of loaves every day, bakers never touch any of them.

Pass round the factory loaf and ask each of the children to read one thing from the ingredients list.

Q: How many things are in this loaf?

A: Depending on the loaf you have chosen, it could be a dozen or more.

Q: What are the other things in this loaf?

A: Some are natural ingredients, the others are known as additives. Most of the loaves that we buy in this country are made using additives.

Q: Does anyone know what any of these additives do?

A: Depending on the additives in the loaf, answers might include to help the loaves rise more quickly, stay soft longer and to stop mould growing so quickly.

Q: Are any of these additives necessary?

A: No. Though each additive has a function, none is actually necessary, as we have discovered by making bread from just [two, three or four] natural ingredients.

Q: Do you think that using additives is good or bad?

A: Though the Real Bread Campaign is against the use of additives, this should be an open discussion. You might choose to set this question as homework, asking children to look at the evidence and collect some of the arguments for and against the use of different additives.

Q: How can you make bread last longer without artificial preservatives?

A: Answers might include:

Freezing. Bread keeps very well if put in a plastic bag or container and kept in the freezer. It is better to defrost slowly, rather than somewhere warm or in a microwave, which can dry it out. Slicing it before freezing allows it to be used one piece at a time.

Using a sourdough starter. The genuine sourdough process generates acids and other compounds that some studies have found can help to delay the onset of mould.

Putting bread in the fridge is not recommended as it accelerates the staling process. Although the low temperature might slow down the growth of mould, if there is too much of a difference between the temperatures of the loaf and the fridge, it can cause condensation to form inside the loaf bag that might have the opposite effect.

Q: What about things that are sold unwrapped in places including small bakeries and supermarkets. Do you think they are like the Real Bread you made or more like the wrapped products?

A: It varies. Some small bakeries make Real Bread, while others use additives. Some supermarkets make some products from basic ingredients on-site, though sometimes using additives.

Some 'freshly baked' products sold at in-store 'bakeries' are made somewhere else, chilled or frozen, and then re-baked in the supermarket when needed. This process is known as 'bake off', which uses around twice as much energy and results in products that can go stale more quickly, which can lead to food being wasted. It is very hard to know which unwrapped products are genuinely freshly baked Real Bread, and which are made using additives and re-baked. The only way to be sure is to ask someone who works in the shop for a full ingredients list and to let you know where the product was made.

Q: What other grains can be used to make flour?

A: There are many possibilities, including:

- Barley (*Hordeum vulgare*). The majority of barley grown worldwide is now used for feeding animals, followed by the production of beer and spirits. Bread made from barley is still found from Europe across to Asia, though. Types include Scottish bere bannock, Finnish rieska and Tibetan balep korkun.
- Buckwheat (*Fagopyrum esculentum*) breads include kuttu ki puri (India) and ajdov kruh (Slovenia).
- Maize (*Zea mays*) also known as sweetcorn. It is native to central America and used for a whole range of cornbreads (e.g. Mexican tortillas) across those countries, as well as through South American countries (arepas), and southern states of the USA. It is also used to make makki ki roti in India and mealie bread in South Africa.
- Oats (*Avena sativa*) are now perhaps better known for making porridge but are also used for making flatbreads in some parts of the UK. Oat breads are also found across northern Europe. Incidentally, the word haversack comes via French from an old Germanic word for a bag for carrying oats.
- Rye (*Secale cereale*) was one a common grain in the UK and is still very popular for breadmaking in Scandinavia, Russia and eastern Europe.
- Rice (*Oryza sativa*) breads include chawal ki roti in India and Pakistan.
- Sorghum (*Sorghum bicolor*) breads include Sudanese kisra and Indian jowar roti.
- Teff (*Eragrostis tef*) is used for injera or enjera, a sourdough flat bread of Ethiopia and Eritrea.

Members of the wheat (*Triticum*) family include durum (*T. durum*), einkorn (*T. monococcum*), emmer (*T. dicoccum*), khorasan (*T. turanicum*), and spelt (*T. spelta*). They are sometimes known as 'ancient' wheats. All can be used to make bread and all contain gluten - in some cases more than modern wheat.

Corn (or sweetcorn) is another name for maize but it's actually an old English word for a grain, hence corned beef (traditionally preserved using large grains of salt), pepper corn and some farmers using it in reference to wheat.

Going against the grain, some breads are made from tubers (potatoes, sweet potato, cassava), legumes, (beans, chickpeas, lentils, peas), and even starch extracted from the pith of the sago palm.

A slice of history

Curriculum subjects

History, geography.

Learning objectives

To find out where wheat was first grown and bread first made.

Q: When and where was wheat first grown?

A: As with many things in history, nobody is quite sure. It's generally agreed that the first type of cultivated wheat was einkorn (*Triticum monococcum*) which literally means one seed/grain. It is thought that this happened in what is now Turkey, perhaps around 10,000-12,000 years ago. It's believed that modern, or bread, wheat (*Triticum aestivum*) was first grown sometime between around 8,500-10,000 years ago. This probably happened in parts of what's sometimes called The Fertile Crescent, which stretches from modern day north Africa into western Asia, including Syria, Lebanon, Jordan, Palestine, Israel, Egypt, and parts of Turkey, Iran and Iraq.

Q: When and where was bread first made?

A: In 2018, charred pieces of something thought to be an unleavened flatbread were found in Jordan and dated to around 14,400 years ago. It was made from pounded roots and wild grass seeds by people from a culture known as Natufian. Similar evidence suggests that sourdough bread might have been made as far back as 10,000-12,000 years ago, somewhere in The Fertile Crescent. The first use of yeast (from brewing) in breadmaking may have begun in Egypt up to around 6,000 years ago.

Q: How much wheat is grown today?

A: Wheat is the second largest grain crop in the word, after maize/corn. China is the largest producer. Around 15.5 million tonnes of wheat are produced each year in the UK, where it is the most grown crop.

Healthy eating

Curriculum subject

Science, food preparation and nutrition, healthy eating, art.

Learning objectives

- The role that Real Bread plays in a healthy diet.
- Where Real Bread sits on the Eatwell plate, and what other foods are in the same section.
- Finding out about food allergies and intolerances.

Materials

The Eatwell plate, which can be downloaded from NHS and government websites.

Introduction

Q: When we first talked about Real Bread, we looked at the main nutrients in flour. What are these?

A: Carbohydrates (mostly starch) and proteins (mostly gluten).

Q: In which section of the Eatwell plate can we find bread?

A: Starchy foods. Starch is a type of carbohydrate.

Q: What percentage of the food we eat should be starchy foods?

A: About a third.

Activity 1

Get the children to write down (and/or draw) as many other starchy foods as they can think of. Answers could include rice, potatoes, pasta, plantain, yam, sweet potato, dasheen, coco yam, kenkey, squash, breadfruit, cassava, breakfast cereals, beans, lentils, peas (and other pulses), couscous, bulgar wheat, maize and cornmeal.

Q: What does the body use carbohydrates for?

A: Mainly as a source of energy.

Q: Bread is also a source of protein. What does this do in the body?

A: Proteins are made up of amino acids, which do many things, including helping to build and maintain cells. They're involved in the immune system, as well as transporting and storing other nutrients. Proteins also provide around the same amount of energy as the same weight of carbohydrates.

Q: Bread also contains fibre. In what way is this good for us?

A: The type of fibre found in bread, especially wholemeal, can help to keep the digestive system healthy. It helps to keep food moving through the gut making us less likely to get constipation. This sort of fibre also helps to make us feel full, which makes us less likely to eat too much food.

Q: What micronutrients do we find in bread?

A: Whole wheat contains many vitamins and minerals, including iron, calcium and vitamins E,

B1, B2, B6 and B12, though a lot of these are removed or destroyed during modern milling to produce white flour. Some are added back into most wheat flour sold in the UK, so bread is a good source of calcium, iron and some B vitamins.

Q: What other nutritional information do food labels include?

A: Levels of fat, salt and sugars. Medical experts advise against a diet that's high in any of these.

Q: Remember the bread that we made? How much salt did it have in it?

A: Each loaf weighed (e.g. 500g) and contained (e.g. 4g) of salt.

Q: Was the amount of salt in our bread less, more or same as the government's target maximum?

A: Less. (Real Bread Campaign recipes produce bread with less than the government's target maximum of 1%.)

As an extra exercise, you could get the students to look at the nutrition labels on a range of loaves – either physically or online at supermarket, price comparison or bakeries' websites. They could check the levels of salt against government guidelines, as well as comparing levels of fat, sugars and fibre between different products.

Q: Why might some people not be able to eat some types of bread?

A: Because they have an allergy, intolerance or auto-immune disease.

Q: What is a food allergy and what is a food intolerance?

A: The body is protected by the immune system. This detects things that are harmful to us, like germs, and helps to get rid of them. If someone has an allergy, their immune system has a fault that causes it to react to something harmless. One type of hypersensitivity causes cells to release histamines that lead to symptoms such as stomach ache, itchiness, a rash or swelling. Other types can lead to tissue damage. A severe allergic reaction, called anaphylaxis, can result in breathing difficulties, high blood pressure or change in heart rhythm. The 14 allergens that most commonly cause reactions include cereals containing gluten (such as wheat, barley and oats), cow's milk, peanuts, sesame, soybeans, and tree nuts.

An intolerance to a food involves the digestive, rather than the immune, system but can cause similar symptoms such as severe stomach ache, vomiting and diarrhoea. The causes of food intolerances vary and not all are well understood. Some are due to deficiency in an enzyme needed for the body to process a certain food or compound in it.

Q: What is coeliac disease?

A: Coeliac disease (pronounced sealy ak) is neither food allergy nor an intolerance, it is an autoimmune condition. This means that the immune system, which is what protects our bodies from illness and infection, starts to attack parts of the body instead of germs. If someone has coeliac disease, eating gluten causes the immune system to attack the gut and can result in damage to the lining of their small intestine. This can reduce the body's ability to absorb some nutrients, leading to deficiency. Symptoms vary but can include stomach ache, vomiting, fatigue, a rash, ulcers, bloating, diarrhoea, loss of balance and more.

Q: What should people do if they think they might have one of these conditions?

A: Don't just Google for a diagnosis and advice! Visit the doctor to arrange a referral to a specialist for tests. Even when family members have similar symptoms, it is important that each person is tested as each could have a slightly different condition that requires different treatment or precautions.

Q: What should someone do if they are diagnosed with a food intolerance or allergy?

A: This depends on the condition and even then can vary from person to person. Some people can simply eat less of whatever is causing the problem, while others have to stop eating it altogether. A specialist might advise someone that they can only eat bread made from particular type or species of grain, with much less yeast, without any additives, or by the sourdough fermentation process.

For more information on coeliac disease, food allergies and intolerances visit: **www.coeliac.org.uk** or **www.allergyalliance.org**

More research is needed

The cultivar of grain that is chosen, how (and with/without which inputs) it is grown, the way it is milled, and the breadmaking process (including use or absence of additives) each may have an influence on how many people can eat it. The Real Bread Campaign calls for much more research to be funded and carried out into the effects of at least the major variables at each stage of the process.

Health and safety

Curriculum subjects

Personal, social and health education (PSHE); food preparation and nutrition.

Learning objective

Thinking about potential hazards in the kitchen/bakery and how to avoid them.

Q: What should we always do before starting to bake or cook and why?

A: Key points include:

- Wash hands thoroughly for at least 20 seconds with warm, soapy water to remove germs, which are microscopic organisms (bacteria, fungi and viruses) that can cause illness.

- Cover any cut with a plaster to stop germs spreading. Ideally, this should be a blue plaster, which will be easier to spot if it falls into food.
- Tie hair back to stop it falling into food and to keep it out of eyes.
- Remove jewellery to stop it falling into food, prevent germs from spreading and keep the jewellery clean.
- Put on an apron to keep clothes clean.
- Wipe work surfaces clean to stop germs spreading and prevent cross-contamination of allergens and flavours.
- If cooking at home, make sure any pets stay away from where we are working to stop germs spreading, hairs falling into food, and to stop them eating it.

Q: What things do we need to do while we are cooking and why?

A: Answers include:

- Clean up any things that have been dropped or spilled to prevent anyone slipping over.
- Don't run, to prevent tripping and/or knocking sharp or hot objects.
- Ask an adult to help when using the oven or sharp knife to reduce risk of burns and cuts.
- Wear oven gloves when putting things into or taking them out of the oven to prevent burns.
- Ensure oven gloves are dry before use, because heat turns water into steam that can scald through the gloves.
- To stop germs spreading, wash your hands each time you enter the room and after you: go to the toilet, pick something up from the floor, touch something dirty (like the bin), or touch your hair or face.
- Don't lick fingers or double-dip a spoon or utensil used for tasting, also to prevent germs spreading.

The evolution of traditional milling

Curriculum subjects

History, geography, design and technology, food preparation and nutrition.

Learning objectives

- History of the development of flour milling technologies.
- Considering pros and cons of different methods.

Materials

This topic is really brought to life if you can get access to different types of mills to use, and/or visit a working mill.

The oldest form of milling was done by pounding grains between a pair of hard objects, such as rocks. This is a brief outline of how it then developed.

Mortar and pestle

Over time, the lower of the two rocks became bowl-shaped and the upper gained a handle, forming what we now call a mortar and pestle. One early example found in southern France has been dated to around 10,000 BCE.

Saddle quern

Later, people began crushing and grinding grain between a flat stone with a shallow curve and a roughly cylindrical stone that was pushed backwards and forwards over it. This idea was developed independently by civilisations around the world, with examples found in countries on every continent (except Antarctica) and representations seen in many ancient artworks.

Rotary querns

The next major development was changing the backwards and forwards movement to a continuous rotation. Over time, querns got larger until they were too big to be operated by hand and were turned by people (often enslaved ones) or animals pushing long wooden beams. Working examples of querns can still be found around the world.

Watermills

The history of using water power for milling goes back so far that nobody can be certain where or when it first began. It's possible that the technology was invented somewhere in the Middle East, from where it was spread by traders and invaders. Another possibility is that similar technology developed independently in a number of places around the world. The oldest remains of a watermill found in the UK were at Ickham in Kent, thought to have been built by Roman settlers in around 150CE.

Water from a stream, river or reservoir/millpond is diverted through a narrow channel called a mill race. The pressure of this flowing water on the paddles of the mill wheel makes it turn. The wheel is attached to a series of cogs and shafts that make the runner stone go around.

Windmills

Windmills operate in a similar way to watermills. The main difference is that instead of the millstone being powered by water pushing against the paddles of a wheel, it is driven by air (wind) pushing against sails. These sails are attached to a cap at the top of the mill which turns so that the sails face into the wind. In the same way that a weathervane operates, a fantail behind and at right angles to the sails keeps them pointing into the wind.

Like watermills, nobody can be sure when or where the first ones were built, though it's thought they might have been in use in Persia (now Iran) as far back as around 500CE. The oldest known references to windmills in the UK date to the 1180s. It has been speculated that the technology may have been brought back by 'crusaders' returning from invasions of, and wars in, Muslim territories.

Q: How do wind and water mills make flour?

A: Grain is ground by two large, circular mill stones, made from hard rock. These lie horizontally a very small distance apart, with the lower or bedstone fixed in place and the upper or runner stone turning above.

Grain is dropped down through a hole in the middle of the runner stone and carved channels, radiating from the centre, carry the grain out to the edges, grinding it as it travels. The coarsely ground flour emerges at the edge of the stones. If finer flour is required, it might be passed through a different pair of stones that are set closer together.

To produce whiter flour, it is sieved (this is known as bolting) to remove the larger particles of bran and germ. Some of the finer particles of these very nutritious parts will always remain in stone-ground flour as they fall through even the finest sieve.

There are records of bolting going back as far as Ancient Egypt, when they used sieves made of papyrus leaves. The Normans introduced to Britain temes, fine sieves made of hair, which allowed more of the bran to be sifted out. It wasn't until the mid-1700s that very fine sieves made of silk began to be used, making the production of even whiter flour more widely available. Today, sieves are usually made of steel or nylon.

Q: What are the advantages of wind and water power?

A: Energy coming directly from wind or water is free, non-polluting, carbon-neutral, does not need transporting and will (theoretically) never run out.

Q: What are the disadvantages?

A: These natural sources of power can fall below necessary strength for days, weeks or even permanently. Wind can drop or can be blocked permanently by new buildings. A millstream can become a trickle in a drought, when frozen in winter, or due to increased use (such as a dam or irrigation system) upstream.

There used to be thousands of mills around the UK. Over time, most of the mills were closed and the ones that are left can only produce a small amount of the flour we need.

Modern milling

Curriculum subjects

History, design and technology, food preparation and nutrition.

Learning objectives

- History of the development of modern flour milling technologies.
- Considering pros and cons of different methods.

Q: How is flour milled now?

A: Most flour used by bakers in the UK, and sold in shops, is produced by high-speed steel rollers that are powered by electricity. There is earlier evidence of metal rollers being used for other milling, but in 1833, Jakob Sulzberger opened the first practical roller mill for flour at Frauenfeld in Switzerland. Roller mills began to be introduced to the UK in the 1860s, initially used in combination with sets of stones. Complete roller mill systems began to be introduced from the 1870s.

Sets of steel rollers break the grain open, strip away the germ and bran and then grind the endosperm to a fine powder. Between each set of rollers are sieves to separate the different parts (fractions), either to be kept for final blending or to be sent through the next set of rollers. At the end of milling, fractions will be blended back together in different combinations and ratios to create a range of grades of flour for different uses.

Stages of roller milling

- Cleaning: Dirt, stones, chaff, insects, plant seeds and any other unwanted bits are removed.
- Conditioning: Moisture levels in the grain are evened out. This makes

separating the endosperm easier and helps to stop the bran breaking up – larger flakes are easier to separate out than finer ones.
- Gristing: Different batches of grain (selected for a range of factors including taste, colour and protein content) are mixed together.
- Breaking: The grain passes through up to four sets of ridged rollers. These break the grain open and split off the bran, endosperm and germ. Sieves after each pair of rollers separate the different parts.
- Reducing: The endosperm is passed through up to twelve sets of smooth rollers. The spacing of each set is closer than the previous one, producing finer and finer particles. Sieves after each set of rollers separate out any remaining bran and channel larger particles of endosperm to the next set of rollers.
- Blending: Fractions, or streams, produced from the endosperm are re-combined in different proportions to create different types of flour. For brown flours, some of the bran and germ will be added back as well. In the UK, wholemeal flour must include all of the fractions in the same amounts and proportions as in the cleaned grain.
- Bagging: The bran, germ and different flours are weighed and packed. Most flour is packed in heavy-duty paper sacks (usually holding 16kg or 25kg) for commercial use.

Only a small percentage of flour milled in the UK is packed in 500g – 3kg bags for use at home. When many people took up home baking during the first lockdown of 2020, industrial millers struggled to keep up with demand for small bags of flour, leading to shortages in shops.

Comparing different milling methods

Q: What does making flour using a mortar and pestle, querns, watermills and windmills have in common?

A: They all use stones to crush the grain to make wholemeal flour. To make brown or white flour, the bran and germ has to be sieved out.

Q: How is this different from modern roller milling?

A: Steel rollers break, separate and individually grind fractions of the grain. To make wholemeal, brown or different white flours, the fractions are re-combined in different proportions.

Q: What are the advantages of stone milling?

A: Because the whole grain is crushed together, even when the flour is sifted to make white or brown flours, it will contain lots of tiny particles of the wheatgerm and fibrous outer layers of the grain.

Q: What are the disadvantages of stone milling?

A: The amount of flour each set of stones can produce in a day is much, much less than a roller mill can. Although nutritious, when the oil in the wheat germ is exposed to air, it spoils relatively quickly, so stoneground flour won't keep as long as roller milled flour. Millstones wear down more quickly than steel rollers and have to be redressed (the channels re-cut) regularly.

Q: What are the advantages of roller milling?

A: Roller mills can produce enormous quantities of flour every hour, much more than any wind or water mill. This helps to make the flour affordable to more people and ensure that there is enough flour for everyone.

Q: What are the disadvantages of roller milling?

A: More of the nutrients in wheat are either removed by roller milling than by stone milling. Generally, the larger the scale of any business/operation, the fewer jobs per unit it supports. The flipside of greater efficiency and economy of scale, which results in cheaper flour, is less employment per kilo. (Note that the idea that roller milling 'destroys' more nutrients on account of heat is very questionable. Millstones tend to heat up and produce warm flour, while rollers are usually chilled/cooled. In any case, heat produced during milling is nothing compared to the oven the flour will end up in...)

Q: What happens to the parts of the wheat that are removed from white and brown flour?

A: A lot of the bran will be sold to make animal feed. The wheatgerm is a good source of vitamin E and can be sold for use in supplements or hair and skin care products.

Q: Why do you think the government controlled the flour that could be made during and after the two world wars?

A: To make white flour, a significant percentage of the wheat grain is removed. By the 20th century, the UK had become reliant on imported wheat for breadmaking. During both wars, many ships carrying this wheat were prevented from reaching the UK. The government wanted to make sure that as much of the limited amount of wheat available went to feed people, not animals, so raised the minimum permitted extraction rate. These browner flours were higher in fibre and more nutritious than white, but produced denser loaves that were unpopular.

Flour 'fortification'

With the exception of wholemeal, all wheat flour sold in the UK has to have minerals and synthetic versions of vitamins added. They are:

- iron.
- thiamin(e) - vitamin B1.
- niacin (nicotinic acid or nicotinamide) - vitamin B12.
- calcium carbonate - chalk (except to self-raising flour with calcium content of at least 0.2%).

Effectively, this means that you cannot buy additive-free white or brown (including multigrain, malthouse, wholegrain, GranaryTM etc.) wheat flour in the UK. As this is a legal requirement, it is an exception to the Campaign's no-additives Real Bread criterion.

When this practice was reviewed in 1981, the government's advisory Committee on Medical Aspects of Food Policy (COMA) reported that the form of iron used was poorly absorbed and most people's intake of the four micronutrients was adequate anyway. COMA recommended the legal requirement for their addition be revoked but this was disregarded. When regulations were reviewed again in 2012 -13, the concerns remained but nothing changed. In 2021, the government announced the mandatory addition of folic acid was to be introduced at some point during 2023.

At the time of writing, the change in law had been pushed back to an unspecified date in 2024, followed by 24 months for mills to comply. Exemptions are due to be made for flour from mills that produce less than 500 tonnes per year, and flour milled from wheats other than *Triticum aestivum*.

In praise of wholemeal

Wholemeal flour is said to be 100% extraction, meaning that all of the hulled and cleaned grain ends up in the flour sack or bag. As well as being high in fibre, wholemeal flour is also high in a range of vitamins, minerals and other micronutrients.

A diet rich in high-fibre, wholegrain foods (such as wholemeal Real Bread) is linked to improved health and a reduced risk of non-communicable diseases, including cardiovascular disease, obesity, type 2 diabetes and some cancers. Studies indicate that wholegrain foods might also support a more diverse, healthier gut microbiome – the unique community of microorganisms that live in each of our digestive systems. A growing body of evidence suggests that the state of your microbiome might have a huge impact on not just your digestive system, but aspects of your wider physical and even mental health.

According to the Department for Environment, Food and Rural Affairs (Defra), however, 91% of bread flour produced in the UK is highly refined. To produce white flour, modern industrial roller mills work at an extraction rate of up to about 82%. This means that at least around 18% of the wheat, which could be used to feed people, ends up elsewhere and might even be wasted. Some stone mills work at lower extraction rates, meaning that even less of the grain ends up as flour. Because the process is fundamentally different (see pages 95 to 99), however, a sifted stoneground flour might be higher in micronutrients and fibre than a roller-milled white.

On the whole, people in the UK do not eat enough fibre: the national average consumption is 20g per day, which is a third less than the UK's 30g reference daily intake and a fraction of the 90g RDI in some countries. In an attempt to make up for some of the removed micronutrients, four (soon to be five) vitamins and minerals must be added to all non-wholemeal flour sold in the UK. This does not replace other discarded micronutrients or lost fibre, and as far back as 1981, the government's Committee on Medical Aspects of Food Policy noted that the iron added is in a form that is poorly absorbed by the body.

Wholemeal on the rise

There has long been a wholegrain/wholemeal bread movement in the UK and elsewhere. Notable historic advocates include Thomas Allinson (the site of whose mill in Bethnal Green is within walking distance of where Sustain's / the Real Bread Campaign's office now stands), and Sylvester Graham in the USA. Encouraging and enabling Britain to eat more wholemeal bread was the main focus of The Campaign for Real Bread (aka CAMREB, one of our Campaign's predecessors) that was founded by the Vegetarian Society in 1976. Focussing on health, nutritional, environmental and flavour aspects, there is a current resurgence of interest in wholemeal bread, particularly in the overlapping Real Bread and non-commodity grain movements.

What's in a name?

According to The Bread and Flour Regulations (1998), for the word wholemeal to be used to name or market bread sold in the UK, all of the wheat flour used must be 100% extraction. In 2022, the Real Bread Campaign began challenging big brands using the word wholemeal to name and market products made with up to 50% white flour. At the time of writing this book a year and a half later, Defra and the trading standards community were telling us they were still working on resolving the issue. Despite our lobbying for a decade and a half, there is still no legal definition of the word wholegrain or regulation of its use.

The language of loaf

Curriculum subjects

English, history, geography, ancient and modern foreign languages.

Learning objective

- To see how words related to bread are in wider use.
- Learning words for bread in other languages and comparing them.

Q: Evidence of the importance of bread includes how it is embedded in the English language. What words and sayings can you think of that include or are related to bread?

A: Examples include:

- Bread = money (literal or rhyming slang - bread and honey).
- Dough = money.
- Bread and butter = main source of income.
- Breadhead = focussed on making money.
- Breadbasket = stomach.
- Loaf = head (rhyming slang – loaf of bread).

Language	Word	Language	Word
Afrikaans	brood	Icelandic	brauð
Arabic	خبز	Indonesian	roti
Basque	ogia	Gaelic (Irish/Scots)	arán/aran
Bengali	রুটি	Italian	pane
Bulgarian	хляб	Japanese	パン
Catalan	pa	Malay	roti
Cebuano	sa tinapay	Maori	taro
Chichewa	mkate	Norwegian	brød
Chinese (simplified)	面包	Persian	نان
Czech	chléb	Polish	chleb
Danish	brød	Portuguese	pão
Dutch	brood	Russian	хлеб
Filipino	tinapay	Slovak	chlieb
Finnish	leipä	Slovenian	kruh
French	pain	Somali	kibistii
German	Brot	Spanish	pan de molde
Greek	ψωμί	Swahili	mkate
Gujarati	બ્રેડ	Swedish	bröd
Hausa	burodi	Welsh	bara
Hebrew	לחם	Xhosa	isonka
Hindi	रोटी	Yoruba	akara
Hungarian	kenyér	Zulu	isinkwa

Common sayings

- Man cannot live by bread alone.
- Staff of life.
- Separating the wheat from the chaff.
- The upper crust.

A bread of loaf?

In Old English, hlaf meant bread and brēad meant a piece of it. Over time, the words evolved into loaf and bread and their meanings swapped over.

- Lord comes from the Old English hlafweard or hlāford, meaning loaf ward - bread guardian.
- Lady comes from the Old English hlǣf dīġe, meaning bread kneader.

Loaf is related to words for bread in other European languages, including:

- Leipä (Finnish)
- Leib (Estonian)
- Хлеб / khleb (Russian)
- Chleb (Polish)

Words that bread is related to include:

- Brot (German)
- Brood (Dutch)
- Bröd (Swedish)
- Brød (Danish)

Pan global

Q: Do you know the word for bread in any other languages?

A: Ask the children to write down as many as they can think of, either individual, in pairs or in groups. You might want to then map the geographic origins of the words. There are more than 7,000 languages in the world, and many more dialects, so these represent just a fraction of the possible answers.

An A to Z of Real Bread

Curriculum subjects

Geography, history, art and design, food preparation and nutrition.

Learning objectives

- Discovering the wide variety of Real Breads from across the UK and around the world.
- Looking at similarities and differences between a range of breads.

Activity

- Children name and/or draw types of bread historically / traditionally associated with your area and other parts of the UK.
- In groups and/or as a class, the children discuss similarities and differences between breads.
- This can either be done off the top of their heads or as homework / a research project.
- If you are able to make or buy examples of any of the breads, children can tray tasting and describing the flavours, aromas, textures etc.
- A great follow-on exercise is to make one or more of the types of Real Bread. Maybe there's someone from your school or local community who has expertise by experience of making one.

The following are just a few examples as inspiration – there are many more. Some breads are still hard to find outside their traditional 'home', though many are now available, made or imitated more widely.

The recipes for many types of bread vary widely, from locality to locality and even from family to family. Many recipes continue to evolve, with vegetable oils often replacing animal fats, for example. All are (or were at one point) made with barm or trub (both forms of surplus yeast generated by brewing), baker's yeast or a sourdough starter. Some bakers now make versions of a number of these using baking powder, which puts those versions outside our definition of Real Bread – see page 7.

Names can be confusing. What some people call pikelets others know as crumpets and people also disagree which bread is a crumpet and which is a muffin…and many people use this last word in its more American sense as a type of cupcake. See also the note about names on page 121.

If there's a Real Bread from your local or regional heritage that you'd like to add to the A to Z of Real Bread on the Campaign website, please email us.

Scotland

Bannock: originally were heavy, flat, unleavened breads, often made from bere (a type of barley), oats or rye and cooked on a griddle. The word is now also used for a range of products including 'quick breads' made using baking powder, and the fruited, enriched dough Selkirk Bannock.

Black bun: is bread stuffed with a deep filling of spiced, dried fruits that are often soaked in whisky.

Butteries or rowies: are flaky, buttery, savoury breads, most associated with Aberdeen. An article in The Guardian said they 'look like roadkill croissants' and quoted film director Duncan Jones calling them 'evil bricks of tasty.'

Wales

Bara: means bread in the Welsh language.

Bara brith: is Welsh for speckled bread. It is sweet, dense, spiced and dotted with dried fruit.

Crempog: a Welsh griddle cake. The word is related to krampoch in Lower Brittany and the English crumpet.

Pikelets (bara pyglyd): are soft, flat griddle cakes, which are like thin crumpets.

Northern Ireland

Aràn: is the Irish Gaelic word for bread.

Aràn pràtaì: is an oven baked bread made with wheat flour and potatoes.

Barm brack: is a sweet, fruited bread, flavoured with caraway. It was originally leavened with barm, the yeasty sediment left by brewing beer.

Boxty: a griddle bread made with a mixture of wheat flour and grated potatoes.

Farl or fadge: a round, flattish bread, made with a deep cross cut into the top so it can be broken into quarters. Historically it was cooked on a griddle, though now is often baked in an oven. It can be made with any combination of white or wholemeal wheat flour, oats and potatoes, and often involves cultured buttermilk. Before chemical raising agents became common in the late 19th century, farls would have been leavened with barm or baker's yeast. Farl means 'fourth part'.

England

Banbury cake: a sweet bread from the Oxfordshire market town, traditionally flavoured with rose water, cloves, mace and caraway.

Bath bun: is enriched with butter, sugar and usually eggs. Various combinations of candied citrus peel, saffron or caraway seeds are sometimes added.

Chelsea buns: Enriched dough, which is spread with sugar and currants or raisins, then rolled up, cut into rounds and proved again before baking. It is thought that they were first made some time in the early 1700s at The Bun House in Chelsea, London, which closed in 1839.

Chudleigh: round white buns, enriched with butter and sugar. Associated with Devon and Cornwall and eaten in the same way as scones.

Crumpet: a small, round, flatbread, about 1-2cm deep. It is made from a yeast-leavened batter of flour and water, which produced many deep holes during cooking on a griddle or hotplate. The name may come from the Welsh word crempog.

Eccles cake: a flaky, enriched sweet bread, filled with spiced dried fruit, which take their name from the Lancashire town. The exact place and date of origin is uncertain, but a bakery is known to have been selling them in 1793.

Floaters (or swimmers): small lumps of bread dough, boiled in soups or stews as dumplings in Norfolk.

Harvest loaf: This is often baked in the shape of a sheaf of wheat to celebrate a successful harvest. It is the continuation of an ancient (originally pre-Christian) tradition, when Lammas (loaf mass) bread was made with flour from the first harvest.

Huffkins: Flat, oval buns, with a deep indent in the middle, from Kent.

Hot cross bun: Spiced, fruited, enriched bun, with a pale cross piped on the top. They are part of the traditional celebrations after the fasting of Lent, though now are often available long before Easter.

Lardy cake: A flaky yeasted bread, enriched with lard, sugar and dried fruit, which perhaps originated in Wiltshire.

Malt loaf: A dense, sticky, fruited bread, sweetened with malt extract and dark sugar or treacle.

Muffin: a flat, round bun, made in a metal ring so the wet dough keeps its shape, and flipped over during cooking. The name might come from the old French word moufflet, meaning soft. Americans call it an English muffin to distinguish it from what they call a type of cupcake.

Oast cakes: Fried barm-leavened dumplings, originally made by hop pickers in Kent.

Saffron bread (or saffron cake): is enriched with sugar, butter and flavoured with saffron and other spices.

Sally Lunn: is another bread from Bath, enriched with egg, sugar and butter or cream, with some recipes being very similar to ones for the city's eponymous bun. It perhaps takes its name from a girl who lived in the city over 300 years ago, or maybe is a corruption of soleil et lune, which is French for sun and moon.

Simnel cake (Britain, Easter but originally baked for Mothering Sunday) Originally a yeasted bread, which took its name from a Roman flour called simila.

Splits: Smaller version of the chudleigh – see above.

Stottie: like a large muffin but baked on both sides on the bottom of the oven, so also known as a bottom cake. The name comes from a dialect word meaning 'to bounce'.

Oatcakes: oat and wheat flour flatbreads associated with Derbyshire, Staffordshire and Wales, where they are soft, whilst in Yorkshire, they may be dried until crisp.

Plum bread (or cake): Sweet, spiced bread. Most (or perhaps all) recipes use dried fruit such as currants, rather than plums.

Teacakes: sweet, fruited, spiced buns. Like hot cross buns but without the cross.

Traditional shapes

The following names are more identified with shapes than particular recipes.

Bloomer: a hand-shaped loaf with rounded ends and several diagonal slashes on the top.

Coburg: round, hand-shaped loaf with a deep cross slashed in the top.

Cottage loaf: a round, hand-shaped loaf with a smaller round on top that has a deep dent in the middle.

Farmhouse: a tin loaf that might or might not have a slash along the top and might or might not be dusted with flour.

Rumpy: a hand-shaped loaf with a chequerboard pattern of slashes on top.

Split tin: a tin loaf with a deep slash along the top.

Bread from around the world

Curriculum subjects

Geography, ancient and modern foreign languages, history, art and design, citizenship, food preparation and nutrition.

Learning objectives

- As well as being an everyday food, Real Bread features in celebrations of many cultures.
- Similarities and differences between bread from different heritages.
- Activity
- Children name and/or draw types of bread with origins outside the UK.
- In groups and/or as a class, the children discuss similarities and differences between breads.
- This can either be done off the top of their heads or as homework / a research project.
- If you are able to make or buy examples of any of the breads, children can tray tasting and describing the flavours, aromas, textures etc.
- A great follow-on exercise is to make one or more of the types of Real Bread. Maybe there's someone from your school or local community who has expertise by experience of making a bread from their cultural heritage.

Notes

Bread may be made special by adding extra ingredients that are (or were at one time) expensive or hard to obtain, such as spices, eggs and butter. Another way of using bread to mark a special occasion or event is by forming it into a particular shape. A third way in which breads might be made for religious use is by making them as simple as possible, like the communion wafer. Some bakers/manufacturers make versions using additives, putting them outside our Real Bread definition.

Here's just a very, very small selection from a world of Real Bread, many of which are now eaten at times and places beyond their origins. Many are claimed by more than one country, known by a variety of names, and made using recipes and methods varying from place to place and even family to family.

(If there's a Real Bread from your cultural heritage that you'd like to add to the A to Z of Real Bread on the Campaign website, please email us.)

Agege bread (Nigeria) Taking its name from a suburb in Lagos state, this soft, sweetish, chewy, white sandwich loaf is typically baked in a lidded Pullman tin.

Arepa (South American countries) Unleavened, thick, muffin-like flatbreads, made from pre-cooked maize meal since long before European invasions began in the 1490s.

Aish baladi (Egypt) Often made from wholemeal wheat flour and circular in shape, these flattish leavened breads are a bit like thicker pitta. The name of this staple means bread of life.

Bagel/beigel (Eastern Europe) Usually made from highly refined, high protein wheat flour. What makes a true bagel more than a roll with a hole is boiling the dough briefly immediately before baking. Their spread around the world is mainly associated with the displacement of communities of Jewish people.

Bolo rei (Portugal, Epiphany) A ring-shaped, enriched bread made with dried and candied fruits and spices. The name means king cake, perhaps in reference to the three magi visiting Bethlehem with gifts for the newborn Jesus.

Brioche (France) Yeast-leavened, white wheat flour dough, enriched with butter, sugar and eggs.

Challa(h) / cholla(h) (Jewish, Sabbath and Rosh Hashanah) Enriched with oil, sugar (and/or honey) and eggs. On the Sabbath, it is usually plaited (the strands mean truth, peace and justice), whilst at Rosh Hashanah (New Year) it is made into a coil with no beginning and no end to signify continuity. The name is Hebrew for 'offering'.

Chapati/roti (South Asia) Round, unleavened, wheat flour flatbread, cooked on a flat pan or hotplate. Some people use the names interchangeably, others make the distinction between wholemeal chapati and refined flour roti. As with other breads from the region, versions of roti have travelled and become established with diaspora in their new homes.

Christstollen (Germany, Christmas) A very rich bread, packed with fruit, nuts and spices.

Damper (Australia) Traditionally baked in a lidded, cast-iron pot, either covered in campfire embers or placed in a hole in the ground and surrounded with them.

Enjera / injera (Ethiopia and Eritrea) A tangy, chewy, sourdough flatbread made from teff flour.

Fougasse (France, Christmas) Branch-shaped flat loaf from Provence, flavoured with olive oil and sometimes with other ingredients such as bacon or anchovies. Now eaten year-round. Like Italian focaccia, it takes its name from the Latin for hearth, focus, as that's where it was originally baked.

Khachapuri (Georgia) Eye-shaped, leavened wheat bread with raised edges, comparable to a pizza. Typically filled/topped with cheese, eggs and other ingredients.

Kisra/kissra (Chad, Sudan, South Sudan) A sourdough flatbread similar to in/enjera but made from wheat, millet or sorghum flour.

Lagana (Greece, first day of Lent) in Eastern Christianity. Unleavened or raised using baker's yeast. Typically oval-shaped with a dimpled surface, sprinkled with sesame seeds.

Lavash (Armenia, West Asia and Caucasus) Thin, leavened or unleavened wheat flour dough, which is roasted on the inside wall of a tandoor (or similar) oven, or on a flat or convex thick metal pan.

Mantou (China) White wheat flour steamed buns, perhaps dating back as far as 300BCE. Steamed buns that are filled, or served filled, are known by names including baozi, or bao for short.

Matzo (Jewish, Passover) This bread is unleavened as a reminder of the story that the Israelites had to leave their leaven behind when they were forced to flee Egypt.

Pan de muerto (Mexico, el Dia de los Muertos - Day of the Dead) This 'bread of the dead' is eaten on All Souls Day (2nd November) to commemorate and celebrate the lives of dead relatives and ancestors. Bread made from wheat flour was historically a luxury in Mexico, where maize was the staple grain. This was further enhanced by enrichment with eggs, sugar and typically flavoured with orange zest, orange blossom water and anise. One estimate is that there might be 1,200 variations of recipe and shape across Mexico.

Pan de sal (Philippines) Rolls of wheat flour dough, dipped in breadcrumbs before baking, giving a crispy golden-brown crust. A popular part of breakfast, traditionally made with slightly pointed tips.

Panettone (Italy, Christmas) A light, golden bread, enriched with eggs, butter, dried fruit and spices. It is often given as a present.

Paratha (South Asia) Layered, unleavened flatbread, cooked on an oiled pan/hotplate. Names, ingredients and methods vary. Some are wholemeal, others refined wheat flour. The layering/lamination is done by rolling and either folding or coiling, depending on the version. Displacement and other migration has led to versions becoming staples elsewhere, including Malaysia (roti canai) and Caribbean countries.

Paska (Ukraine, Easter) Yeast-leavened sweet bread, enriched with eggs, sugar and butter. Similar breads (often with additional spices, dried fruits and even chocolate) are found across Eastern Europe.

Paximadia (Greece) Double-baked, sourdough bread made from barley, rye, wheat or mixed flour and enriched with olive oil. Usually softened with water or olive oil before eating.

Pide (Islam, Ramadan) Although eaten all year round, this low-rise, circular bread is traditionally associated with Ramadan, when Muslims only eat once a day after sunset.

Pita/pitta (Mediterranean and Middle Eastern countries) A family of leavened flatbreads with prehistoric roots, usually made from wheat flour. Round, oval or tear-shaped. Many versions can be cut or torn to reveal a pocket that can be filled.

Pizza (Italy) Naples claims to be the origin of what we know as pizza today but pizza shares culinary and linguistic roots with a whole family of flatbreads, including pita and pide. By the 20th century, pizza had gone global and has been reinvented in many ways, perhaps most notably in the USA, where numerous cities each have their own distinctive styles.

Pogača (Croatia) From a family of Balkan breads of the same name, the version from the Dalmatian region of Croatia is a huge (sometimes 5.5kg), round, wheat loaf, made for sharing. Traditionally baked on a hearth under a bell-shaped peka with embers piled on top.

Pulla (Finland, Christmas) Enriched with eggs, sugar, butter and often flavoured with cardamom. It is now eaten all year, often as buns to go with coffee.

Sacramental bread (Christianity, Holy Communion) After it has been consecrated, bread signifies (or, to some people, literally becomes) the body of Christ. It is eaten, alongside a sip of wine to represent his blood, during the ceremony of Communion/Eucharist as a reminder of the belief that Jesus sacrificed himself for mankind. Depending on the strand of Christianity, the bread (known as host) is either leavened or unleavened and in some branches of the church has become stylised into a small, thin, unleavened disc.

Shokupan (Japan) Soft, white wheat flour milk bread, often baked in a lidded Pullman tin. The fluffy texture is largely down to the yudane method of mixing some of the flour with boiling water, which gelatinises the starch, then mixing with the other ingredients once cooled.

Simit (Turkey) Yeast-leavened, white wheat flour bread in the shape of a twisted ring. Often dipped in sesame seeds before baking.

Vetkoek (South Afrika) The Afrikaans name for a deep-fried, yeast-leavened, white wheat flour, savoury doughnut. Crispy on the outside, soft and fluffy on the inside, the name literally means 'fat cake'. In Zulu and Xhosa they are called amagwinya or magwinya.

Zopf (Switzerland, Austria, Germany) Similar to brioche, though typically with added milk or cream and made with less butter and egg.

Further notes for teachers

Working space

If you have a dedicated food technology space or access to the school canteen's kitchen, great! Otherwise, are any of these alternatives viable options for you?

Mixing can be carried out in a classroom or school hall. Classroom tables are fine to use as work surfaces if they are cleaned thoroughly first. A two-stage process is advised – warm water with a very small amount of detergent, followed by clean water to prevent soapy loaves.

- The canteen of local business or organisation.
- A bread machine.
- Pupils take the dough home to bake. Only really an option if they make it at the end of the school day. Also bear in mind that not every family will necessarily be willing or able to turn an oven on to bake a bread roll.
- Flat breads using a griddle/pan on a portable stove.
- Building an outdoor oven in the school grounds.
- Borrowing/hiring a small oven, of the type used by microbakeries or for event catering.
- Borrowing/hiring a portable wood-fired pizza/bread oven.

If you are considering either of the last two options, there is a chance that your visiting baker might have such an oven. Otherwise, we suggest that you ask parents and the wider school community network, or you can search on the Internet. If breadmaking is to become a permanent fixture on your school's timetable, you might consider running a crowdfunding campaign to buy an oven, or to build an outdoor oven.

Another thought – is taking a group of children off-site for a breadmaking lesson at a local bakery or baking school a workable option for you?

Example lesson plans

There are many ways that Real Breadmaking can be woven into a primary school morning/afternoon, full day or starting one day and finishing the next. As with everything in this book, one size doesn't fit all, so here are a few ideas that might help you decide how Real Breadmaking will best fit into your day.

A period during which bread is left to do its own thing (rising/proving and baking) can be scheduled to coincide with a break time or other lesson, with the children continuing with the next stage afterwards. Other options include cleaning/tidying up, a theory session (perhaps from the Lessons in Loaf suggestions), children tending to their Bake Your Lawn plot or taking notes and measurements for their wheat diaries; or something creative. We've seen two approaches to the idea of 'bread and jam'. One involves drumming, singing, songwriting or other musical activity while the dough is rising. The other is literally making jam or other preserves – from the school garden, if you have one.

A morning of Real Bread

Back in 2010, Andrew Wilson of Different Breid in Glasgow told us: "My class involves two batches of dough, one I take with me and one the pupils make." This is based on notes Andrew sent us:

8:00: I make the first batch of dough at the bakery allowing 500g flour per pupil plus one portion for me.

8:15: The first batch of dough is divided into batches for its first rise.

8:30: I drive to the school.

9:00: Each pupil gets a Real Breadmaking kit; 500g flour, 350g water, 10g yeast and 8g salt (plus spatula, dough scraper, apron, bowl and tea towel - all in a large kraft paper bag with handles, that's good for taking the bread home in.)

9:15: The pupils and I each make dough and put into bowls to prove.

9:25ish: We divide the first batch of dough and shape into loaves.

9:40ish: Have a bit of a clean up and everyone goes for their first break.

10:15: We use the dough we made in the classroom to make fougasse.

10:30: The batch one loaves and batch two fougasse are baked.

10:40: We all have a good clean up and I have a cup of tea.

11:10ish: The loaves are taken out of the oven and left to cool down.

12:00: Bread ready for eating at lunchtime or taking home. Any spare dough from fougasse stage can be bagged up and taken home.

"Everyone gets a copy of the recipes and methods. There is plenty of time during and between stages for questions and showing pupils bubbly/smelly sourdough cultures. Pupils tend to really enjoy a break from more academic stuff and are very attentive/well behaved, which is a bonus."

Real Bread in a day of cooking

This is based on a lesson plan that Virtuous Bread and Bread Angels founder Jane Mason has used in schools, which includes making other recipes during the time the Real Bread is proving.

9.15-9.45: Introductions and a short discussion about bread, baking, what kind of bread they like, what it's made of etc.

9.45-10.15: Weigh out and knead ingredients for the Real Bread. Leave it to rise.

10.15-10.30: Break time.

10.30-11.00: Make soup from scratch and put it on to cook.

11.00-11.30: Clear up.

11.30-12.00: Shape the Real Bread and leave it to rise.

12.00-13.00: Have lunch.

13.00-13.30: Clear up and put the Real Bread into the oven.

13.30-13.45: Make pancake batter.

13.45-14.00: Take the Real Bread out of the oven and let it cool.

14.00-14.30: Fry and eat pancakes.

14.30-15.00: Clear up.

15.00-15.15: Review the day, talking about what they learned and what they enjoyed.

Jane said: "The most important thing is to fill the gaps while the bread is rising and baking. These gaps are LONG if you are 10 or under." She went on to say: "An alternative to making pancake batter is to make jam so they can all take home a little pot of jam. Or they can make cookies or anything else quick. We do a lot of clearing up. It is a good opportunity to get them to work in teams and a great opportunity to praise and thank. Everybody has to wash up his or her own bowls and spoons and pans and they take turns sweeping the floor and cleaning the counter tops."

From flour to sourdough in a week

Here's a way to schedule the dough monster and sourdough Real Bread (pages 58 to 61) across a week.

- Monday morning: Theory lesson and children begin the dough monsters.
- Tuesday, Wednesday and Thursday mornings: Children feed their dough monsters.
- Thursday afternoon: You (or a Real Bread baker) guide the children in making dough, which is then left in the school canteen fridge to prove overnight.
- Friday morning: The children shape the dough and leave to prove.
- Friday afternoon: The bread is baked in the school ovens, after lunch service and clean up.

A Real Bread baker could be involved in one of several ways, for example visiting:

- to run the theory session on Monday, then again for the dough mixing and finally for the baking.
- only for the mixing or baking session.
- on the baking day to begin a different, short-process bread from scratch, which will get baked later that day for the children to take home.

More thoughts

- Out to lunch: If you're able to use the school canteen's ovens, you will need to come to an agreement with the caterers about when you will have access. It is likely that this will be in the afternoon, after the kitchen team has cleared up following lunch.
- Here's one I made earlier: Dough is brought to the lesson by the baker for children to shape. While the shaped dough is proving, the children make a second batch of dough from scratch. The first batch is baked at school (and perhaps eaten on site, maybe for lunch), and the second batch is either baked later in the day or given to the children to take home to bake.
- We'll be back after this break: Make dough in the last lesson of the morning and leave it to prove over the lunch break. You then shape and leave it for the second proof. This might tie in well with the schedule of the school canteen. Some long-rise recipes allow plenty of time between stages for other lessons and break times.
- Daily bread: If you can dedicate a whole day to bread, the hands-on stages can be interspersed with experiments and regular lessons in which you use bread as the topic for each subject – maths, history, geography etc. You could extend this over a period, either consecutive days or one day per week. Either would allow related class visit(s) to a bakery, farm or mill. A regular breadmaking

session would really help to consolidate skills and confidence.
- Take away: Instead of baking at the school, children take their dough home, along with baking instructions. This is made easier if you have silicone-lined card bread 'tins.' You can find suppliers of these by doing an Internet search. Alternatively, dough can be taken home in sealed plastic containers, where children reshape it and leave it to prove again before baking. Plastic bags can be used but it can be tricky to get all of the dough out.
- Night working: Longer fermentation doughs can be started during the last lesson of the day and left to prove overnight. The children then shape the dough next morning and the loaves are baked when proved.
- Flat out: Typically, flat breads will have shorter proving and cooking times than risen breads, so can be made in a relatively short time using minimal equipment.

Who'll run your Real Breadmaking session?

If you would like to find a professional Real Bread baker willing to teach a breadmaking class and/or talk about working in a bakery, a good place to start your search is the Real Bread Map on the Campaign website. Perhaps your school has a teacher with food preparation and nutrition training.

Other options might include:

- A cook/trainer from your catering provider or local authority.
- A tutor/teacher from a baking/cookery school on the Real Bread Map.
- You or another member of the school's teaching staff. If wanted or needed, you could take a class or a course with someone on the map to build up your knowledge and confidence first.
- Someone else from the school's network (parents, governors, past pupils and so on), or wider local community, who is confident in being able to teach the children to make Real Bread.

Who'll do what?

If the breadmaking session is being run by someone other than a member of school staff, we recommend a meeting (or at least a conversation) to discuss how the session will run and agree who will be responsible for what. Ideally an advance visit with a tour of the facilities will be arranged.

We suggest that points to be discussed and agreed should include:

- Date of the session.
- Timings of the session to fit in with the school day.
- How much set-up and clean down time is needed.
- How many pupils will be participating in the breadmaking.
- Where and when the Real Bread will be made and baked.
- Equipment and facilities needed, and who will be responsible for providing each item.
- Ingredients needed for the Real Bread being made, and who will be providing and paying for them.
- If the school will be covering any of the visitor's expenses – a contribution towards travel to/from the session, for example.
- Who will print off recipe sheets.

Other considerations:

- Vehicle parking or public transport options for the visitor.
- Will pupils eat the bread at school or take it home and, if so, in what?
- Has the class done (or will be doing) any work tied in with the breadmaking session?
- Checking and accommodating any food allergy or other dietary requirement in the group.
- It is a good idea to exchange mobile phone numbers in case of any problems on the day.
- If any child has an individual learning assistant, their presence at the session will be very helpful.
- Are there any teaching assistants or parent helpers who could join in with the breadmaking? As well as providing extra support for sticky hands, they could find it an enjoyable learning experience themselves.

You and the baker might choose to put the agreement in writing.

DBS checks

We recommend that anyone who visits your school to provide or assist with any of the activities suggested in Bake Your Lawn is always supervised by a Disclosure and Barring Service (DBS) checked member of school staff. The same applies for any offsite visits, such as to a farm or bakery. Unless the visitor is being paid or making more than three visits in a 30-day period, they do not need a DBS check, though your school policy might require one. Note that these notes are not legal advice and you should check official sources for current legal obligations and good practice guidance.
www.gov.uk/dbs

Support

A number of national websites can help schools, charities and community groups find grants for projects. An Internet search can also help you to find regional and local funding opportunities.

You could also consider running a crowdfunding campaign, perhaps with the help of your school's PTA. We have heard from schools that have funded raised beds, gardening equipment and even ovens to set up microbakeries in this way.

When it comes to digging, sowing, weeding and harvesting, maybe friends, family or other members of your local community might agree to lend a hand. This is particularly helpful if you are planting anything more than a few square metres. If you are planning to cultivate a small field, the offer of some of the resulting flour, or bread baked from it, in return might be an appropriate gesture of thanks. Maybe a local business or organisation might lend (or perhaps even donate) gardening equipment to you.

UK bakery market

The bakery market can be measured by volume (number of products sold) or value (sales turnover). Depending on whether and which industry figures you choose to believe, perhaps around:

80% (figures range from 75% to 85%) of the loaves sold in the UK are produced by eight industrial manufacturers at 25 highly automated factories. Half of these loaves are produced by just three companies. The wrapped, sliced loaves are made by the Chorleywood Process, a high-speed system that involves a cocktail of additives and larger quantities of yeast than Real Bread bakers typically use.

15 –17% of loaves come from supermarket in-store bakeries. Though production may involve input from bakers with craft baking skills, the loaves might still contain additives not used by Real Bread bakers. A growing number of in-store 'bakeries' merely re-bake products that were made elsewhere.

3 –5% of loaves are made by what are commonly known as 'craft' bakeries. There is no legal, or generally accepted, definition of craft bakery - even the Craft Bakers Association doesn't appear to give one on its website. While some 'craft bakers' make only Real Bread, others use additives.

An honest crust?

You can't always rely on the label for the whole truth about an industrial loaf. For example, if a manufacturer asserts a substance is a 'processing aid', they can choose not to let you know it has been used, let alone what it's called or its origin.

A supermarket (or any other retailer) can market products using claims like 'freshly baked', 'made throughout the day', 'freshly baked', 'baked here today', when in fact they were made a long time ago, far, far away, and merely re-baked in what the Real Bread Campaign calls a 'loaf tanning salon'. Other than certain allergens, retailers can choose not to display ingredients lists for food they sell unwrapped.

Historical authenticity

It can be argued that the only way to create truly 'authentic' versions of historic Real Breads would be with a time machine. This would be the only way that you could use exactly the same ingredients and equipment. As you don't have a working TARDIS (if you do, please get in touch) you will have to make compromises; how many and to what extent will depend upon the time available, and how close to replicating all details you feel is appropriate.

Some thoughts:

- Most of the wheat varieties grown in the UK are modern, dating back no more than a few decades.
- Before the 19th century, rye, oats or barley were more commonly grown than wheat in many parts of the UK.
- Where wheat was grown, it was usually in a mixed crop with other cereals (such as rye, oats or barley) known as maslin or monks' corn.
- Historically, the wheat varieties grown in Britain tended to have a lower protein content, producing flour that would have been suitable for lower rising breads (crumpets, muffins, focaccia, ciabatta and baguettes are made with softer flours) rather than high-rising tin loaves.
- Roller milled flour was introduced in the 1830s, was first produced in Britain from 1872 and took many years to become widely available.
- The use of brewer's yeast began in the late 1600s and the production of compressed (AKA fresh) baker's yeast was not perfected until the mid-19th century.
- Fast-acting yeast was not introduced until the early 1970s and not widely available until the 1980s.

- Petrochemical fertilisers, pesticides and herbicides were virtually non-existent before World War II.
- Domestic ovens started to become more common in the mid-1800s but many homes did not have ovens until well into the 20th century.

These are just some reasons that you might feel that older cultivars of 'ancient' grains (for example spelt, einkorn, emmer, barley, rye); stoneground, organic flours; barm (surplus yeast generated by brewing) or a sourdough starter are more appropriate when trying to recreate historic recipes.

Similar arguments apply to making an 'authentic' version of a bread associated with a particular place. Can and should a loaf be called San Francisco sourdough if it was made anywhere other than SF? Even if made using imported French flour, should a baguette manufactured (for example) in Croydon by Polish bakers be called French bread?

Chemical raising agents

We include this because many people have asked us over the years why we don't publish recipes that involve baking powder. It's great to see people making their own cakes, biscuits, scones and so on but products made using chemical raising agents fall outside the Real Bread definition used by the Campaign, Real Bread Ireland and others.

Dead end

With our interest in the known and potential benefits of longer fermentation, chemical raising agents are a tangential cul-de-sac away from a line between unleavened flatbreads, via breads leavened using baker's yeast, to genuine sourdough. Chemical raising agents work by an almost instantaneous chemical reaction between an acid and an alkali. The resultant fizz inflates dough in seconds, without any of the beneficial (and potentially beneficial) changes that occur during fermentation.

Coeliac link?

The Campaign doesn't suggest that chemical raising agents are unhealthy. It's interesting to note, however, that some studies have found higher than global average levels of coeliac disease amongst people in Ireland. Further research is needed to discover whether this is in any way linked to half a dozen or so generations of Irish people frequently getting stuck into chemically leavened loaves, purely genetic, or a combination of factors.

Sounds like

In challenging the Campaign's position the likes of 'soda bread' and 'cornbread', some people make the argument: 'if it has bread in its name, then it must be bread'. Names, though, are a linguistic convention, which don't always tell you what a thing actually is. There also can be inconsistencies: banana bread is a cake; saffron cake is a bread; shortbread is a biscuit; and laverbread is mush of boiled seaweed. In Scotland, and oatcake is a biscuit, while in parts of central and northern England, it's a type of flatbread. What an American would call a biscuit, most Brits would call a scone. Incidentally, we can safely say that a jaffa cake is a cake (for VAT purposes, at least) thanks to a 1991 court ruling against Her Majesty's Revenue and Customs, which had argued the jaffa cake was a biscuit.

It is perhaps also understandable that similarities in the ways soda and sourdough are sometimes pronounced can lead to people confusing the two.

Tradition

Another common argument used in support of chemical raising agents is tradition. Rather than being some ancient custom, though, their use began in the mid-to-late 1800s. Before this, everything was unleavened or raised by one form or another of yeast, so it could be argued that Real Bread traditions trump any claim made behalf of nineteenth-century newcomers.

We don't use tradition in our argument, mainly because it's such a slippery concept. Where, when and what other criteria should be used to determine whether or not something is traditional? Is having been habitual for a certain period necessarily evidence of something's validity or intrinsic value?

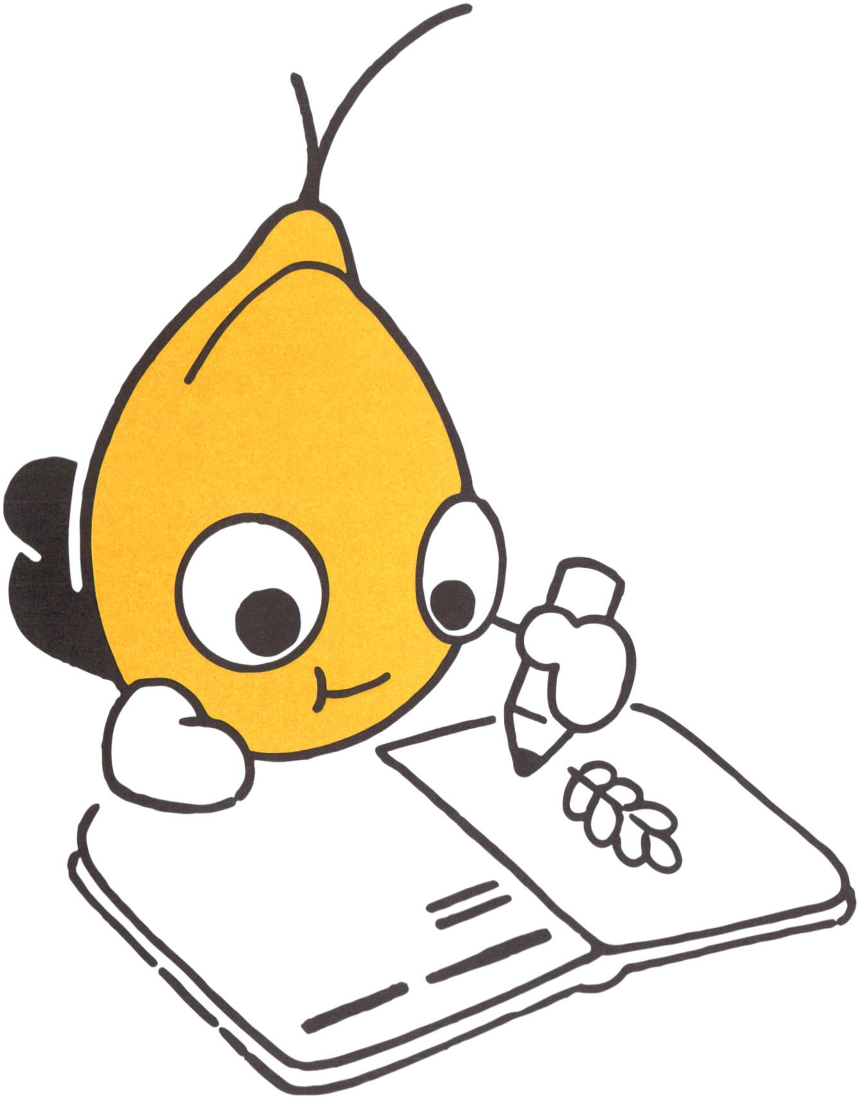

Wheat diaries

When we ran the original Bake Your Lawn project from late 2010 to early 2013, we asked participants to send us brief updates of how they were getting on. Here is a small selection of entries that might help to inspire you, with a few that might console you if things aren't going quite as you'd expected...

March 2011

"Jack (5) and Charlie (3) have baked a lot of bread and sourdough before (Jack shapes a mean loaf) and they're excited to have their own field. Charlie in particular was very keen on the seeds we sprouted in a jar and insisted on planting those too! With permission, our field is in the garden of the empty house next door and they check it most days. They think it is funny that it looks like grass. On the recommendation of Secular Homeschooling (an American magazine), we've ordered Bread Comes to Life: A Garden of Wheat and a Loaf to Eat, so we're looking forward to that arriving." **Sarah Dickinson, home educator, Northern Ireland.**

"The children (all 240 of them) have sown their wheat. Each of the eight classes has an area of about one square metre. The first seeds were sown on Friday 11th March and, thanks to a lovely open plot and some sunny weather, the first shoots were poking through the soil in just over a week. Looking at the little rows of green spikes one child commented 'Look! They're beautiful.'" **South Harringay Junior School, London.**

April 2011

"Jack and Charlie have been measuring the shoots against all sorts of different things to keep track of how it is growing. We have plans to team up with our local school to do something exciting when we come to mill it and, if we can, I want to build a cob oven in our back garden to bake our bread in. We have a sourdough culture already, so it will be very, very Real Bread!" **Sarah Dickinson, home educator, Northern Ireland.**

May 2011

"This is on a small plot on Lower Drayton Farm in Staffs. The chicken wire is an attempt to keep out the rabbits. The ground originally had pigs on it so I suppose you could say we used the pig tractor method to prepare the ground. We're lucky to have the farmer on hand to advise us. He's told us that as the seedlings are so close together (broadcast sowing) they will have smaller seed heads. We're hoping to sow a few neat rows in different soil for comparison." **Home educator, Staffordshire.**

"Our community trainees prepared the ground late March and the following week pupils from two of the local primary schools visited to plant the seed. By early May this is looking great and growing really strongly. The area planted forms part of the much larger Community Gardens lottery-funded project, which aims to involve the local community in growing and eating better. Plans are developing to build a clay oven to bake the bread made at community bake sessions." **Meadow Well Connected Community Centre, North Shields.**

"We are an inner-city primary school in London's east end. We are developing an edible playground and your wheat is a big part of that! We have it growing in the playground garden as well as by a class in their roof top planter. It's doing well! We plan on visiting a miller when it is ready and to ask a local baker to come and help make it into a loaf." **Chisenhale Primary School, London.**

"We planted the wheat at our secondary school at the end of March and have been keeping records of its progress. We plan to harvest the wheat when it's ready and the food technology department are going to take it from there. The wheat's planted right outside the school canteen so all the students can watch it grow. It has grown an amazing 7cm in two weeks!!" **Great Marlow School, Marlow, Buckinghamshire.**

"We are growing our wheat in our school garden in the middle of Glasgow. We don't actually have any garden as such, everything that we grow is grown in pots and containers." **Garnetbank Primary School, Glasgow.**

"We are currently growing wheat in one-metre square beds at our school. Years 3 to 6 have planted the seeds in slightly different ways and will be interested to see which method produces the most seed at the end of it. Recent rain has meant a growth spurt, I just hope that the wheat will wait until after the holidays in the summer before it can be harvested." **Berkswich Primary, Stafford, Staffordshire.**

"We have sown wheat in eight-foot circular bed. Unfortunately some of the rows have not germinated but we have wheat. We have used it in the sensory garden and hope it will blow and grow, sound windy and look like a waving sea of grass alongside the herb garden and touch bed." **Penn School, Buckinghamshire**

"The children from our school will be measuring their corn on Tuesday next, 17 May, at the school allotment in Ely, Cardiff, in the afternoon. One of the pupils,

Zach, will be talking about the Bake Your Lawn project on Radio Cymru's Dafydd a Carol show on Wednesday morning." **Ysgol Gymraeg Treganna, near Cardiff.**

"We have just planted our wheat and made bird scarers. We are hoping that it will be ready to harvest when we come back in September. We want to harvest it, mill it and bake it and try to tie this in with our harvest festival celebration." **Northfield Junior School, Derbyshire.**

"We planted 12 square metres of wheat and the plan is to have the kids back at the end of summer to harvest, mill and bake it. We have just finished building an earth oven at the garden too, so we really can take the kids all the way from seed to loaf." **Abbey Physic Community Garden, Kent.**

June 2011

"A Bake Your Lawn demonstration was established at Ryton Gardens in spring 2011. This is centred on a plot of Paragon, a modern spring wheat variety. There were initially problems with birds causing damage to the young seedlings and so we protected them with fleece. This was very effective and a good population of plants was established. We were also able to water the plot several times during the dry weather. Now, in early June, the plants are just beginning to show ears. In an adjacent plot we are demonstrating some of other cereals. We had a patch of rye that was sown in the autumn as a green manure. We have allowed this to grow on to produce grain and it is now well over five feet tall! We also sowed some heritage varieties of wheat, oats and barley that we were sent by Mike Ambrose of the John Innes Centre in Norwich. This complements an adjacent display of our own Heritage Seed Library varieties of vegetables.

We hope to be able to feature the project in events at Ryton later in the year. About half an acre of Paragon wheat was also sown in our research field so that we would have more material to use in possible threshing and milling demonstrations. It will be interesting to compare the yield of this wheat with that grown in the gardens under much more intensive conditions." **Garden Organic, Ryton Gardens, Warwickshire**

"The garden had just been revamped and we decided to plant our seeds in a 1m x 1m plastic raised veg bed. We prepared the veg bed and planted our seeds on 6th April - a lovely sunny warm day. We have been checking on the growth and watering. As of half term (Monday 30th May) our wheat is still doing well - the three rows are different sizes, ranging from 28cm to 36cm. We know a farmer who is going to loan us some millstones so hopefully we can produce our own flour at the end of this venture." **The Eco Team, Peatmoor Community Primary School, Swindon**

July 2011

"The children have planted about a square metre of wheat in their allotment in Pontcanna Fields. Luckily the allotments are opposite a riding school, so there is always plenty of manure available. We planted two old varieties, one Welsh and the other Swedish. We planted a row of each variety separately and two rows of mixed seeds. We weighed the seeds as we put them in and will try to weigh the amount of grain we get from each row when we harvest them. The Welsh variety seems to be taller but the Swedish variety stands up straighter, they are about five feet tall." **Cardiff Woodcraft group**

"We planted the wheat on 5th May, just throwing handfuls of seed over ground we had weeded and raked. Then we raked the seeds in, watered them and covered the soil with a net so that the birds could not eat them. We were very excited to start measuring it on 17th May as we had not expected it to be through so quickly! Here are our measurements: 17 May, 7cm; 24 May, 24.4cm (what a difference some rain makes!); 7 June, 30cm; 14 June, 35cm; 21 June, 39cm; 4 July - 85cm. The children are really enjoying this project." **Northfield Junior School, Derbyshire.**

August 2011

"Today, seven children from the class that planted the wheat (plus siblings, friends and parents, an LSA and a teacher) took time out of their summer holidays to harvest our wheat. It was a glorious sunny day for the cutting and the threshing. We thoroughly enjoyed it and learned more about wheat farming in the process. Farmer James was a huge help, showing us exactly what we needed to do." **Takeley Primary School, Hertfordshire.**

September 2011

"The reception pupils planted their mini-wheatfield way back in March and watched it steadily grow, measuring the height occasionally, right up to the summer holidays. The summer ripened the wheat and when we came back to school in September it was ready for harvesting. The children, now in Year 1, harvested it two weeks ago. They cut the ears and rubbed them above a sheet to remove the grains. We then had a go at winnowing, even though it wasn't very windy, tossing everything in the sheet to separate the grains from the chaff. We then separated out some grains and crushed them using various methods (stones, rolling pins etc.) to see the flour inside. Before the end of October, the children will be visiting Butser Ancient Farm, taking some wheat with them, to find out how wheat was ground into flour in Celtic times using quern stones. We will then be baking bread during their next cookery lesson." **Petersgate Infant School, Clanfield, Hampshire.**

Wheat diaries

"The Garden Club successfully grew a square metre of wheat. It was harvested and is now drying in a pillowcase. It may even be being bashed (threshed) as I write this! The local press are coming to photograph it being milled next Monday, so there will be a little report in the paper. The club has been very enthusiastic and benefitted from the experiences." **Dines Green Primary School, Worcestershire.**

"The Park is a school for 100 students with learning difficulties. We grew the wheat (a patch about 1m by 3m) on our allotment near our food technology room. During various lessons (enrichment, horticulture, gardening club) throughout the summer we looked at and talked about the wheat growing. The wheat lodged during the summer holidays due to the wet weather but our groundsman harvested it and left to dry. Since the start of the autumn term, students have gathered it into a sheaf to use in our harvest assembly. Our food tech teacher is going to bake bread in a lesson, then stand it with the wheat." **The Park School, Surrey.**

"Against all the odds, our wheat has managed to grow. The Key Stage 3 gardening club sowed three rows of seed a little late - right at the end of lunchtime on 7 April, our last day before going off for Easter! We scraped three furrows along the top of a mound of bare, dry soil at the far corner of the school field. As the bell was sounding, we rapidly tipped in the carefully weighed-out seed, and then hurried to the buildings to wash hands and get to lessons.

We then had absolutely no rain for several weeks. To our amazement, though, some of the plants in the top two rows germinated and looked quite strong when we went off for the summer. A further long period of dry weather followed, but we returned this term to find ripe ears of wheat. Three of our pupils, who have only been in England for a few months, harvested it. I asked if they knew what it was and they replied 'naan'. Clearly, they have seen naan making at all its stages. We laid the wheat out to dry in a wicker basket and this week we shall separate out the grain using the pillowcase and brick wall method! Or we might try walking on it." **Tile Hill Wood School and Language College, near Coventry.**

"We split the wheat so that two-thirds were grown in the metre-square raised bed and the remaining third grown on an allotment with plenty of space. Sadly, the wheat grown in the raised bed was affected by the early heatwave we had. Although it grew to over 50cm high, it didn't have a very good yield of wheat when we harvested it in September. We wondered whether it was because the root system went only 5-6cm into the soil. The allotment-grown wheat fared better but again was affected by the hot weather in the spring.

We would like to repeat the experiment next year if possible and would like to set up and investigate how different growing media affect the growth and yield of the crop. After learning from my mistakes this year as it's been so enjoyable and interesting for the students taking part. After a research lesson they were amazed at what products were made from wheat and how much maths is needed." **Great Marlow School, Marlow, Buckinghamshire.**

"Our Year 3 children sowed the seed in late April in a small, raised bed, covered it with netting to keep birds and animals off and watered sparingly as the weather was very dry. Germination was slow and patchy but eventually it virtually covered the bed. Progress has been observed by each group of gardeners - the children take turns to look after the small garden. Our other crops this year included lettuce, radishes, Swiss chard, sweetcorn, small squash and ornamental gourds. We cut the wheat three weeks ago using long-handled shears, rolled it into a large sheet and it is now drying on my dining room floor. Some of the wheat will be used for decorating the village church for harvest. We plan to thresh it at school and have arranged with our local windmill that the children (now Year 4) will be able to grind it using the mill's querns. This means a morning visit to the windmill with a walk across the Ashdown Forest to get there. We hope to have a baking session, though it is unlikely that we will have a significant amount of our own flour. We are all enjoying taking part in the project." **Nutley Primary School, East Sussex**

"We have been making the most of our cob oven in our school garden. The children have made bread on several occasions and used breadmaking within the science curriculum, looking at yeast for changes. The children also make delicious pizzas, which they cook outside in the cob oven with one of our dads." **Longtown Community Primary School, Herefordshire.**

"All is going well so far. We've harvested (children with scissors!) and threshed. Inspired by Roald Dahl characters, we have made a BFG scarecrow, complete with a little Sophie, and had our photo in the papers." **Tintwistle Primary School, Glossop, Derbyshire.**

"I grew two patches of wheat. One was in a community garden with school children in Dunton. The germination was very patchy and we didn't get enough to do anything with but we enjoyed growing it! The other was a smaller patch on an allotment but a mouse (and her babies) were living in the compost heap and ate the lot!" **Dunton Community Garden, Bedfordshire**

"We really tried to grow a loaf of bread on the roof garden. It all started off so well with beautiful green shoots that our gardeners were so proud of but the weather, and probably the fact that we only had a very shallow bed to sow the seed in, were against us. We had a square metre of wheat and it was going great guns, then the terrible winds and rains bashed it all to the ground.

The students were so keen to go the whole way to spreading our bread with homemade jam. We still have some grain left so will try again next year and try to find a deeper bed, maybe in a different area of our school, which doesn't have the crazy microclimate that our roof garden has. Thanks for giving us the opportunity to take part. We really enjoyed it." **Haberdashers' Aske's Hatcham, London.**

"We're harvesting now, a rare patch of sunshine and all the wheat seems golden and ready. We'll see how we go from here! Jack and Charlie are bringing home the harvest! Okay, it's not a lot but a reasonable bag-full and we're pleased! We enjoyed looking at wheat grains and different sorts of flour, coarse and fine, through magnifying glasses." **Sarah Dickinson, home educator, Northern Ireland.**

"The harvest at Sarehole Mill Museum has not been very successful because the pigeons got there first. I thought our very young visitors (reception and Year 1 children) had been somewhat enthusiastic in their hands-on approach, only to find a large flock of pigeons early one morning devouring what was left of the wheat. However, I have decided that growing wheat on site is a definite must and will certainly do it again next year. We have been able to pick some of the wheat, grind it and bake it." **Sarehole Mill, Birmingham.**

"I had turned about 1.5 square metres into a small, raised bed. The wheat was sown in March with 3-4 seeds per hole, 15cm apart. The wheat grew really well! At the Castle Garden party, after the climbing competitions and whilst the DJ was pumping out some house music, I harvested the wheat using my Austrian scythe, which took all of three strikes! People then helped to put the wheat into bundles. On 1 September we threshed it with the help of three of our garden volunteers, using pillowcases and whacking it against the wall, as well as hitting it with a mallet! We then winnowed it, pouring it from bucket to bucket in the wind to blow away the husks, as well as hand-picking stalks out. It took a few hours and a bit of work. However the end result was about 1.17kg of wheat! Next stage is to get it milled and made into mini pizzas and focaccias." **The Castle Climbing Centre, London.**

October 2011

"We had a fantastic morning grinding and baking here. Children from four of the schools in the Bude Friends of the Earth Local Growing Schools group gathered together on Tuesday 11 October. We winnowed and ground the wheat they had grown on a saddle quern, a rotary quern and finally in an electric flour mill. We also started up the waterwheel of the mill and talked to the children about how we will be able to grind flour in the mill once the wallower has been replaced and 100 wooden teeth are made for the pit-wheel. We then mixed the dough (with a bit of extra flour added from Doves Farm) and the children cooked individual pieces wrapped around sticks over a fire. The rain held off, the sun came out, and the bread was yummy - especially as it was dipped in toffee! Thanks for organising the project - it was great fun." **The Bridge Mill, Devon.**

"Growing a loaf of bread! Each class was involved - there are two classes in each of four years and 30 kids in each class. We planted the wheat in April and harvested in September. In October, we threshed the wheat (beat it in a pillowcase against the wall until all the grain had fallen out of the husks), winnowed it (blew away the chaff until only the good grain remained) and milled it in Mr. Banham's coffee grinder. On 14 October we baked our flour as bread and ATE IT. DELICIOUS! Maren, Kirsty, Vanessa, Shelley and Lucy all helped the garden club cooks to produce bread and cakes for the whole school." **South Haringey Junior School, London.**

"We had a lot of willing hands, including cousins, grandparents and aunts, so we did OK with the mortar and pestle. We didn't have a huge amount to grind and it certainly gave the children a real idea of the physical effort involved in making a loaf of bread – or in this case some rolls! We're using a sourdough that Jack and Charlie helped make so the whole experience has been pleasurably basic and hands-on. Homegrown, home-ground wheat, homemade sourdough starter, salt and tap water. Unless we dig a well and evaporate our own sea salt you can't get much more homemade! They really have been involved in every single aspect of the creation of their lunch. The rolls are proving now. We've also made some traditional plaits with the wheat and talked a lot about it all." **Sarah Dickinson, home educator, Norther Ireland.**

"We grew four square metres of wheat from about 100g of seed sown in March. We harvested a reasonable size sheaf, threshed it etc. ground it up ended up with 400g of flour - just enough for a loaf, and what a loaf it is. We made it in school today ready to show at our harvest festival tomorrow. We're quite pleased with ourselves. The children have a new-found admiration for farmers and bakers, but more importantly were blown away by the process of making and eating their own bread. We made five loaves using some shop flour but one loaf from our own flour made from wheat grown at school. Our Year 4 class of 32 pupils ate four of the loaves in 15 minutes and are all set to go home and have another go. Brilliant campaign we loved the experience, but my coffee grinder probably won't recover." **Berkswich Primary School, Stafford.**

"Squirrels ate ours. Soooo disappointing!" **Capital Growth team, allotment training garden, The Regent's Park, London.**

November 2011

"We got a local baker into the school today and had an amazing day. Thirty year 4 pupils took a whole day to firstly mill the wheat, which we had harvested in August. We grew about a kilo of wheat, so I think we did really well!!!! We used a fan on the roof and the children held the bowl of wheat and the light chaff blew away (well all over the children, which they loved) and they were left with the berries. Then they spent the rest of the day making the bread. We made bread rolls for whole class and it was delicious. We would love to do it again next year." **Chisenhale Primary School, London.**

"Having harvested our wheat we separated out the grain using various dubious methods, much to the amusement of a girl who speaks little English but clearly had far more idea than we did! The following week we put the grain in a coffee grinder. All went well for a while but then smoke began to come from the grinder. Perhaps we had dried our wheat too much? We finally sieved out the flour and sent it home with the girl to use in cooking some naan! We now have far more admiration for those people for whom making their own bread is part of their normal day-to-day routine." **Tile Hill Wood School, near Coventry.**

"We are working with five local schools, giving each responsibility for a 6m x 3m plot of land. The pupils tested the soil, prepared the ground and planted the wheat by the broadcast method. They are returning during the year to monitor its growth. When ripe, they will harvest the wheat, leave it to dry, separate the wheat grains from the stems by threshing (a pillowcase and the wall), winnowing the grain to remove the chaff (hair dryer experiment) and grinding the grain using a coffee grinder or we'll take to Green's Windmill. They'll then use flour to bake wholemeal bread for tasty sandwiches or a scrummy pizza or pizzas using the Farmeco outside kitchen." **Farmeco Community Care Farm, Nottinghamshire.**

"Our work with Farmeco has meant that our young people have had some once-in-a-lifetime experiences. They have begun to see themselves as part of a bigger picture, where they have responsibilities as well as rights; and they have begun to understand that they have a part to play in the way that our planet is shaped." **Wings East School, Nottinghamshire.**

December 2011

"Because of the weather we harvested a little late and lost part of the crop. After drying out the stalks the children had a great time threshing, winnowing and grinding in an old coffee grinder. We have about 450g of flour, just enough for a loaf to share." **Cardiff Woodcraft Group.**

"Every stem was cut with a pair of scissors and then we threshed it in pillowcases. We borrowed a quern stone from Stainsby Mill (part of the Hardwick Estate), ground our wheat and then made a loaf. Every child ate some of the bread and said it was lovely, in spite of saying before that they did not like brown bread! The miller from Stainsby Mill came in one day and talked to all the children about the mill and the quern stone, which they found very interesting. We have thoroughly enjoyed this project and may well grow wheat again in the future." **Northfield Junior School, Derby.**

April 2012

"We have planted! As a Food for Life flagship school, we have a really good relationship with our local, organic farm. Our Year 5 children buddied with reception pupils and they went together to plant the wheat on the farm. The farm manager, who is also a governor of our school, chose an area visible from the road to school and that our children will walk past to get to the woods for forest school activities. The wheat is covered with green fleece to accelerate growth, so it makes the area even more obvious for our children to see. Our aim is for Year 5 to harvest, make flour and then make bread with reception children." **Mrs. E. Ditton, Nacton C of E VC Primary School, Suffolk.**

"We are growing the wheat as part of our Year 3 gardening club. There are 14 girls (aged 7 to 8) in our gardening club, which is run by two teachers. We planted the wheat about five weeks ago and it's doing really well. We prepared the soil by removing the weeds and digging it over." **Mrs. Collins, Burgess Hill School for Girls, West Sussex.**

"Our Year 3 classes were keen to grow wheat as part of their Vikings topic, so here they are with their efforts so far." **Juliet Birch-Machin, Stocksfield Avenue Primary School, Newcastle, Tyne and Wear.**

"So far, seven of the twelve schools in the group have planted wheat I had kept back from last year. We have finished restoring our mill to working order, so will be grinding the children's wheat by water power in the autumn." **Rosie Beat, The Bridge Mill, Devon.**

"Today, we started our Real Bread experiment! We sowed wheat seeds in one of the raised planters on Shacklewell Road, so by the end of the summer we should have a mini wheat field that we can harvest, mill into flour and bake into (a small loaf of) bread." **Somerford and Shacklewell Tenants and Residents Association, London.**

May 2012

"We have planted Amaretto wheat, provided by St. Albans farmer Howard Roberts, and the first shoots have begun to appear. Redbournbury Watermill, which is a mile from Howard's farm, has agreed to mill the wheat for us and let us visit for a guided tour with tea and buns on 7 June. We will also be visiting the farm that day, where we will see the workings of the farm then walk through the fields down to the mill for our tour in the afternoon. Watch this space for the finished results!" **Dig Deep community allotment, South Oxhey, Hertfordshire.**

"This wheat seems to be growing inches every day in this sunshine! Kit (18 months) is an enthusiastic waterer, while Jack and Charlie (5 and 7) are keeping the 'field' free from the peas that want to climb up the wheat, instead of the supports!" **Sarah Dickinson, home educator, Northern Ireland.**

"We planted our wheat at the end of February and germination was pretty good. By early May we have half a dozen rows of good strong wheat! The wheat is a central feature of our developing garden area. We were lucky to be given a number of timber planters by a local garden centre and these have been put around the wheat. These will be planted with peas, beans and salad greens. We now have rhubarb and strawberries growing alongside." **Adrian Clarke, Bedlington Day Centre, Northumberland.**

"Our wheat is about 10cm high now. In June we (all 18 of us – it's a v. small school) are going to visit the local Caudwell's Mill in Rowsley to see how flour used to be milled. We'll buy a bag of flour and bake it on our return. I'm not certain our wheat will ripen, but if it does, we've to find a way to grind it." **T. Hodgson, Biggin C of E Primary, Derbyshire.**

"Our school caters for students with a wide range of special educational needs. We raked our plot, picked out the stones and made furrows to drop the seeds in. The first signs of our wheat appeared during the Easter holidays and it is now growing well. The students who planted the wheat were in an environment lesson but a range of students throughout the school will be involved in the project, working in the gardens during gardening lessons, and hopefully making the bread in a science lesson." **Lucy, Ravenscliffe High School and Sports College, Halifax, West Yorkshire.**

June 2012

"On a rolling rota, all children are involved at our school in a gardening club, which meets on Friday afternoons. Along with our other plots and garden areas, the wheat 'field' has become a very popular feature with the children and they are hopeful we will see it produce a small crop in the autumn term." **Harry Kennedy, Black Horse Hill Primary School, Wirral.**

"Sadly, our wheat growing was not a great success. We did all the right things but did not take account of the ducks and coots on the pond adjoining our allotment. They had a great, healthy breakfast one day and thoroughly enjoyed the highly nutritious wheat shoots! We'd like to try again next year using some protective net covering. In the meantime, Donald and his friends say thanks for the feed. I guess it's a trip to buy some bread flour." **Susan Walton, Bishopstone CE Primary School, Swindon, Wiltshire.**

July 2012

"We planted our wheat in our school garden, we were quite late planting - it was early April. However it has caught up and is growing strongly now. The children weeded it in May, then left it. We haven't had to water it! The Garden Clubbers were very excited to see the ears of wheat appear!" **Caroline Copleston, Anthony Roper School, Eynsford, Kent.**

"The wheat is coming on great. Despite the best efforts of the floods and high winds, it is standing up well and the grains are developing and swelling very well. We check on progress most days and weed a little around the edges when it's needed. We are now looking ahead to harvesting and having a celebration picnic outside for the gardening club and their carers!" **Adrian Clarke, Bedlington Day Centre, Northumberland.**

September 2012

"We harvested today! Jack and Charlie did great work cutting the wheat and carefully bundling it up to dry out. We took one head and took it to pieces to see the different parts." **Sarah Dickinson, home educator, Northern Ireland.**

"What can I say?? Our wheat was great before it was ripe but something happened through the summer and it has either been eaten by mice or slugs (as has a lot of our produce) or so wind-blown there is very little grain left, which is so sad. We will definitely be making bread but will have to buy the flour now, sadly." **Diana Keens, Otterham School, Camelford, Cornwall.**

October 2012

"Well, we've had an incredible summer, despite the weather. The wheat field has grown fantastically, some frogs have arrived in our pond and our clay bricks have cured in the newly rebuilt cob oven." **Dig Deep community allotment, South Oxhey, Hertfordshire.**

"We set aside one of our raised beds in the garden, sowed organic wheat and then, rather naively, just left it over summer. Surprisingly, we had a good crop when we returned, so set about the harvest, threshing and winnowing. The wheat was ground into flour by visitors at our school open evening and then baked once the sourdough starter was good enough. The bread was brown to look at, with a lot of bran in the flour, but everyone agreed amazingly tasty. The whole thing was organised by our Years 7 and 8 pupils, who got very enthused by the whole process!

What is important for us as a school is that we have an ethos of closed-loop-thinking. We teach the pupils to mimic cycles of nature as far as possible, so that manufacturing processes of any kind have as little energy loss as possible and that there is no long-term waste. Growing our own bread on site, from seed to loaf is a classic example of low-food-miles, organic production and one we will repeat next year, as we have saved enough seeds from the harvest to start again, closing the loop. Thanks for the inspiration for this. As EcoSchool's first secondary Ambassador School we are now telling other schools how easy it is to do it themselves!" **Mark Moody, The Skinners' School, Tunbridge Wells, Kent.**

November 2012

"Adam, the baker from The Pavilion Café and Elliot's, came into school to run our Lesson in Loaf. The children have grown and harvested their own wheat and today was the day to turn it into loaves of bread!" **Cassie Liversidge, Chisenhale Primary School, London.**

"We have a patch of rye and a patch of spelt growing at school and are planning on a patch of barley, too. This year is only a pilot to see where the issues are and to work out how well we can integrate the project into the curriculum. Learnings to date: our soil is poor and poorly drained. Need to work on that. Students are keen, but we have to develop activities to maintain their interest." **Chris Stafferton, Geneva Christian College, Latrobe, Australia.**

December 2012

"A group of six-year-olds harvested wheat with the tale of the little red hen ringing in their ears. This was thanks to the Real Bread Campaign, whose Bake Your Lawn project had encouraged us back in the spring to plant wheat grains in a long bed next to the basketball pitch. A Noah's Ark summer followed and we feared the worst but, against expectations, our crop did grow and ripen on schedule. Now we're just building up to milling and baking. The Campaign's encouraging suggestion that a friendly local mill lend their services is a little optimistic for our über-urban school, but we're hoping that a food processor will do the trick." **Linden Groves, Hollickwood Primary School, London.**

January 2013

"We had a very successful time making our Real Bread with a kilo of our own homemade flour. In September we harvested our crop in fine weather. We tied it in bunches and hung it to dry in the shed. After drying, we threshed the wheat to separate the ears from the straw. Next we winnowed the wheat to separate the wheat berries from the chaff. Finally, we milled the wheat in a coffee grinder to make it into flour. We had fun making the bread! We are very proud of our finished loaf. Maybe next time we will make some butter and jam to put on it. I made a PowerPoint of our project with the 60 pupils who took part. We showed this in our harvest assembly so that the whole school, a large primary of 450 children, and some parents, knew what we were up to. Well done to all of Year 4 who were involved in the breadmaking process, which started when they were in Year 3 and ended just before we broke up for Christmas. Everyone thoroughly enjoyed the project and we hopefully taught the children a great deal about Real Bread." **Mrs Birch, Stocksfield Avenue Primary School, Newcastle.**

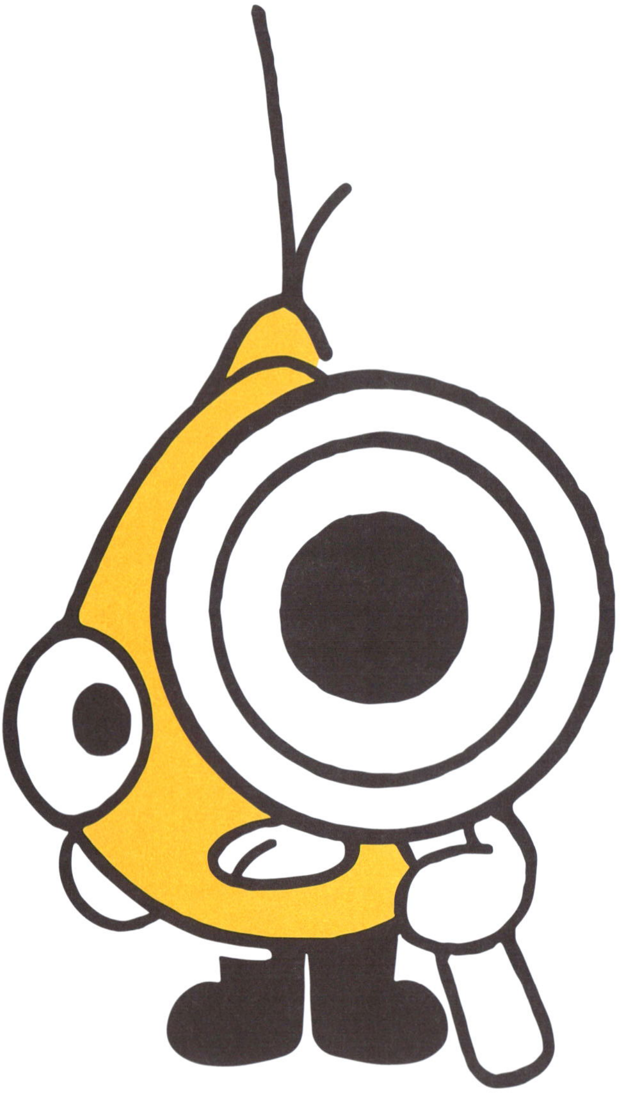

Find out more

Here's a non-exhaustive list of sources of information that you might find useful on your mission to grow your own Real Bread. Some go way beyond what you need for a small project at home or school, into the territory of self-sufficiency and community wheat growing.

Inclusion doesn't necessarily indicate a recommendation by Sustain / the Real Bread Campaign, while there are many great resources and products out there that we've missed or just don't have space to include. Online search engines and marketplaces, as well as yer actual libraries, shops and people's brains, can help you find more.

Grain and growing

Agriculture and Horticulture Development Board (ADHB): A host of commercial growing information including a wheat disease management guide. Note that sections of this involve agrochemicals that organic and small-scale growers would not use.
https://ahdb.org.uk/knowledge-library/wheat-and-barley-disease-management-guide

Britain and Ireland Community Grains Association: Promotes the growing and eating of alternatives to modern bread wheat. The website includes maps of small mills and regional grain networks.
www.bicga.org.uk

The Brockwell Bake Association: A cornucopia of information about wheat, cereal growing and milling. Maintains resources including a database of seed banks.
www.brockwell-bake.org.uk

Grown in Totnes: Information on setting up a small-scale grain community enterprise, including guidance on planning, growing, harvesting, processing and marketing.
www.grownintotnestoolkit.co.uk

Organic Research Centre: A wealth of information, guidance and more on organic, permaculture and agroforestry systems. Also at the centre of landrace, mixed population and other non-commodity grain research.
www.organicresearchcentre.com

OrganicXseeds: The official UK database of organic seed suppliers
www.organicxseeds.com

Regional grain networks: Clusters of growers, millers, bakers, academics and others with interests in non-commodity grain economies. At the time of writing, they were Common Grains (Scotland), Cotswold Grain Network, East Anglian Grain Alliance, South East Grain Alliance, South West Grain Network, The Welsh Grain Forum, West Midlands Grain Network, Yorkshire Grain Alliance.

Scotland The Bread: Member-owned, community benefit society working towards a sustainable, fair supply of flour that better nourishes people and planet. Runs projects and training around growing, milling and baking.
www.scotlandthebread.org

The Sheffield Wheat Experiment: Community arts project helping people to sow, grow, harvest, mill and bake wheat. They're produced a short growing guide, if you're finding this book a bit much!
www.thesheffieldwheatexperiment.co.uk

UK and Ireland Seed Sovereignty Programme: Run by Gaia Foundation to help growers improve diversity of crops and other domesticated plants.
www.seedsovereignty.info

UK Grain Lab: Informal network of non-commodity grain enthusiasts, founded by Kimberley Bell of the Small Food Bakery. Organises a bi-annual gathering in Nottingham.
www.ukgrainlab.com

Homegrown Whole Grains: Grow, Harvest, and Cook Your Own Wheat, Barley, Oats, Rice, and More, Sara Pitzer Storey Publishing LLC, 2009

Small-Scale Grain Raising: An Organic Guide to Growing, Processing, and Using Nutritious Whole Grains, for Home Gardeners and Local Farmers, Gene Lodson, Chelsea Green Publishing, 2009

Southern Small Grains Resource Management Handbook, G. David Buntin and Barry M. Cunfer (eds), the University of Georgia and Auburn University Agricultural Experiment Stations and Cooperative Extension Services (reviewed 2017)
https://extension.uga.edu/publications/detail.html?number=B1190&title=southern-small-grains-resource-management-handbook

Wheat: The Big Picture: In-depth information and images for the entire life cycle of the wheat plant.
www.cerealsdb.uk.net/cerealgenomics/WheatBP/Documents/DOC_WheatBP.php

Mill

The SPAB Mills Section: Offers histories of and other information about traditional mills. Organises the annual National Mills Weekend.
www.spab.org.uk/spab-mills

Steve Overthrow: Understood to be the only traditional sievewright left in the UK.
www.riddles-sieves.co.uk

The Traditional Cornmillers Guild: Its network includes custodians and millers of many of the UK's working traditional wind- and water-powered flour mills.
www.tcmg.org.uk

Various: Brands of tabletop mills include Hawos, KoMo and Mockmill.

Water and Wind Power, M Watts, Shire Publications, 2000

Bake

Bakery Bits: Sells small-scale milling and baking equipment.
www.bakerybits.co.uk

Forno Bravo: Free plans for building your own wood-fired bread/pizza oven and a community forum for sharing advice/information.
www.fornobravo.com

Real Bread Campaign: You can find many places to learn breadmaking skills (some of which cater for children) on the Campaign's Real Bread Map.
www.realbreadcampaign.org

The School of Artisan Food: Runs baking and food business classes and courses.
www.schoolofartisanfood.org

Build Your Own Earth Oven, Kiko Denzer and Hannah Field, Chelsea Green, 2007

Building a Wood-Fired Oven for Bread and Pizza, Tom Jaine, Prospect Books, 2011

The Bread Builders: Hearth Loaves and Masonry Ovens, Daniel Wing and Alan Scott, Chelsea Green, 2011

When we were researching **Lessons in Loaf** in 2010, almost all of the baking books for children we found focussed almost entirely on cakes and biscuits. Since then, things have improved slightly for people seeking ones that focus mainly on Real Bread. Examples include:

Baking Bread with Children, Warren Lee Cohen, Hawthorn Press, 2008

Making Bread Together, Emmanuel Hadjianreou, Ryland Peters & Small, 2014

The Bread Pet: A Sourdough Story, Kate DePalma and Nelleke Verhoeff, Barefoot Books, 2020

Sourdough Baking with Kids, Natalya Syanova, Fair Winds Press, 2021

While not specifically for children, we can't miss this chance to plug our recipe book **Slow Dough: Real Bread**, Nourish Books, 2016

More for schools / teachers

Adopt-a-School: Run by the Royal Academy of Culinary Arts, the scheme arranges school visits by chefs and other hospitality professionals to pass on Real Breadmaking, and other food, knowledge and skills.
www.royalacademyofculinaryarts.org.uk/what-we-do/adopt-a-school

Capital Growth: A Sustain sibling to the Real Bread Campaign, which coordinates a network of community food growing spaces in London and provides support, events and training.
www.capitalgrowth.org

Chefs in Schools: Help to put chefs into school kitchens, as well as offering food education and healthy eating training and guidance to schoolteachers and cooks.
www.chefsinschools.org.uk

Food For Life: Helps schools to put good food on the menu and on the timetable – in and out of the classroom.
www.foodforlife.org.uk/schools

Garden Organic: Offers food growing guidance for schools.
www.gardenorganic.org.uk

Grow Your Own Playground: Runs food growing projects in London schools. Partnered with the Campaign on Lessons in Loaf: London.
www.growyourownplayground.com

LEAF Education: Helps schools deliver curriculum-linked learning through food and farming experiences, both in and out of the classroom.
www.leaf.eco/education/leaf-education

Learning Through Landscapes: Can help schools develop their grounds for gardening and growing schemes.
www.ltl.org.uk

School Food Matters: Offers guidance and training in food growing, education and entrepreneurship.
www.schoolfoodmatters.org

Social Farms and Gardens: Charity offering training and guidance on food growing education and arranging farm visits.
www.farmgarden.org.uk

Royal Horticultural Society (RHS): Provides information on a range of home and school food growing / gardening projects.
www.rhs.org.uk

A Collection of Proverbs of all Nations on Bread and Baking, J.H. Macadam, MacLaren & Sons (1924). Reprinted by Balkankult Foundation, 2006

Another shameless plug: If you fancy exploring setting up a microbakery enterprise, as a number of people have done in schools, and many more in their own homes, our book **Knead to Know…more**, Sustain, 2021 is a good place to start.

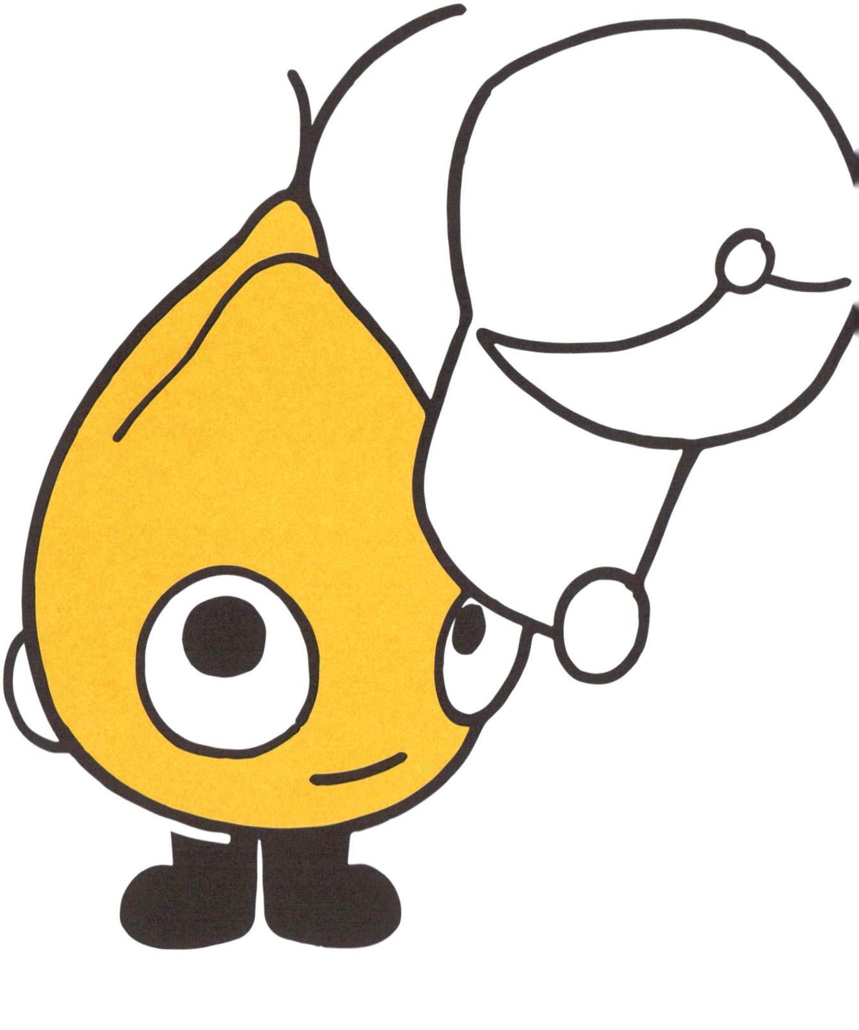

Roll of honour

Bake Your Lawn
by Chris Young and the Real Bread Campaign
ISBN 978-1-903060-68-1

This edition first published in 2024 by
Sustain: the alliance for better food and farming.
244-254 Cambridge Heath Road, London E2 9DA
realbread@sustainweb.org
www.sustainweb.org
www.realbreadcampaign.org

Copyright © 2024 Sustain / the Real Bread Campaign.
Lessons In Loaf is a trademark of Sustain / the Real Bread Campaign.

Except as stated otherwise, text © 2024 Chris Young.

Illustrations © 2024 Lara Durham.
Design and layout by Alan Karlik.
Typeset in Sentient and Apfel Grotezk. Printed in England by Chapel Press.

The right of Chris Young to be identified as the author of this text has been asserted in accordance with the Copyright Designs and Patent Act of 1988. All rights reserved. No part of this book may be reproduced or transmitted in any form or by any electronic, digital, manual, photographic, mechanical or other means, or by any information storage and retrieval system, without permission in writing from the publisher.

To seek permission to copy, reproduce or redistribute any part of this guide, please email **realbread@sustainweb.org**

Knead to Know...more

This book builds on the Bake Your Lawn and Lessons in Loaf projects run, and accompanying guides published, by the Real Bread Campaign in 2010 and 2011. They were funded by The Big Lottery's Local Food Fund, Sustain and The Sheepdrove Trust.

As with those guides, and everything else the Campaign does, this book was a team effort. Chris thanks everyone who variously volunteered their time and utterly indispensable knowledge, advice, opinion, wheat seeds, packaging, distribution, design skills, recipes, proofreading and other assistance to the original projects, guides and this book. They include: Mike Ambrose, Lisa Asuncion, Paul Barker, Lyndsay Cochrane, Idris Caldora, Gemma Cope, Lianna Court, Kath Dalmeny, Raeoni Daly, Tyra Dempster, Gavin Dupée, Ellen Hanceri, Marcia Harris, Tom Herbert, Chris Lindop, Cassie Liversidge, Jane Mason, Dragan Matijevic, Sarah Moore, Liz Read, Jackie Schneider, Anna Soumeka, Patrick Thornberry, Alexandra Vaughan, Gerda Janse van Vuuren, Tom Walker, Georgina Webber, Gaye Whitwam, Andrew Wilkinson and Andrew Wilson.

Elements of the original Bake Your Lawn guide drew on teachers' notes created by The Brockwell Bake Association, whose founder, Andy Forbes, also contributed additional information and advice to our guide and this book. He remains a leading figure in the UK's non-commodity grain revival.

Thanks to Anne Parry, Mrs. Birch, Linden Groves, Chris Stafferton, Mark Moody, Claire Eckley, Malcolm Williams, Sarah Dickinson, Diana Keens, Nicola Jennings, Ida Fabrizio, Caroline Copleston, Adrian Clarke, Harry Kennedy, Sam Maydew, Susan Walton, T. Hodgson, Lucy Ravenscliffe, Mrs. Ditton, Mrs. Collins, Juliet Birch-Machin, Alex Basham-Collins, Rosemarie Parker, Rosie Beat, Francis Rayns, Maria Lewington, and everyone else who took part in our original Bake Your Lawn and Lessons In Loaf projects and shared their wheat diaries with us.

Chris also thanks: his family for ongoing love and support; Jeanette Longfield, Charlie Powell, Ben Reynolds, Quoc-anh Tran, Richard Watts, Sarah Williams and the rest of the Sustain family present and past; all Campaign ambassadors, supporters and volunteers over the years; and you for buying this book.

Last but not least, thank you to Andrew Whitley, who coined the name Bake Your Lawn, contributed to the original guide and most of our work since, and without whom the Real Bread Campaign wouldn't exist. Chris is sorry for not giving due credit to anyone he's missed off this list.

Crowdfunders

Publication of the first edition of this book was made possible thanks to 185 lovely people who chipped into our Crowdfunder campaign in July 2023, who we namechecked on our website. They included:

The Welbeck Bakehouse

Steve Bath, Graham Capper, Mark Diacono, Peter Doughty-Cook, The Fermentarium, Michael Grant, Prue Leith, Gareth Maloney, Ana Reynolds, Dan Sicklen, Morgan Richmond-Watson, Paula Watson, Adelaide Young.

Best Food Forward at The School of Artisan Food, Stephen Brown, James Doig, Eszter Faulkner, John Harris, David King, Steven Moschidis, Andrew Sharp, Marcel van Brakel, Sara Ward, Christopher Wooding, Boudicca Woodland, Ian Woodroffe.